tomorrow brings memories

Tomorrow Brings Memories

Detroit's First Underground Record Company

by Craig Maki

WAX HOUND PRESS

Also by Craig Maki:

"Detroit Country Music: Mountaineers, Cowboys, and Rockabillies" with Keith Cady
University of Michigan Press, 2013

Tomorrow Brings Memories — Detroit's First Underground Record Company

Words, images, cover, and book design copyright © 2022 Craig Maki, except where noted. All rights reserved.

The photograph printed across pages 28 and 29 copyright © Detroit Historical Society, all rights reserved. Thanks to DHS for permission to include it here.

This book may not be reproduced, in whole or in part, including illustrations, in any form (beyond that copying permitted by Sections 107 and 108 of the U.S. Copyright Law and except by reviewers for the public press), without written permission from the publisher.

Edition

Published by Wax Hound Press
Beverly Hills, Michigan, U.S.A.
WaxHoundPress@gmail.com

WHP-101

ISBN: 978-0-578-36442-1

contents

DEDICATION 1

PROLOGUE 2

1. SHOUN BROTHERS 7

2. SHADES OF AN UMBRA 12

3. EDDIE THE IMMUNE 17

4. UNIVERSAL RECORDING STUDIOS 23

5. MARQUETTE MUSIC COMPANY 31

6. YORK BROTHERS 35

7. HAMTRAMCK MAMA 40

8. NEVER BE FORGOTTEN 45

9. HAVE A LITTLE TALK 52

10. IT TAIN'T NO GOOD 55

11. SNAKE BITE BLUES (UNIVERSAL'S LAST YODEL) 58

12. WAYNE COUNTY BLUES 61

13. THE HOT AND MELLOW YEAR: HOT 65

14. THE HOT AND MELLOW YEAR: MELLOW 75

15. MELLOW SONGS TO REMEMBER 81

16. MELLOW TIMES 85

17. BEYOND MELLOW 93

18. EAST SIDE BOOSTERS 99

POST SCRIPT 104

DISCOGRAPHIES 108

ACKNOWLEDGMENTS 127

"Tomorrow brings mem'ries of days that have gone"
  — *York Brothers*

dedication

Little did I know in 1998, when Detroit record dealer Cap Wortman lended me a plain cardboard box containing Universal, Hot Wax, and Mellow 78 rpm records from his personal collection, that a quarter-century later I'd write this book. I was twenty-seven years old, and the contents of the box (the music, as well as the physical discs) presented a mystery that soon grew into an obsession. From the first conversations I shared with Cappy, I realized that collecting rare discs went hand-in-hand with discovering the true, and often peculiar, stories behind them. Thank you, Cappy.

prologue

At the end of the 20th century, Detroit, Michigan, boasted a musical history — a high achievement in itself, comparable to the region's defining growth produced by lumber barons, stove makers, auto manufacturers, and mortgage empires — that competed with the sound legacies of Kansas City, Los Angeles, Nashville, New Orleans, and Memphis.

Astonishing amounts of money circulated across Southeast Michigan via auto manufacturing, construction, agriculture, office work, education, and the arts. Detroit residents celebrated their lives with musical entertainment thrown at house parties, performed in restaurants, theaters, festivals, nightclubs, and on radio and television. The number of records that originated in Detroit could fill a skyscraper of the imagination up to a penthouse with sounds from big bands to small jazz combos, to high school students making chart-topping pop music; from factory workers waxing blues or country songs they'd written between shifts, to religious groups of all kinds and sizes seeking to spread the gospel; from rock and punk, to hip hop and techno. How high must the roof rise? How deep might stacks of discs draw us in, inviting us to find the first trickles of this stream of music? Let's try one hundred years.

In 1921, when the *Detroit News* reported breaking stories, and broadcasters played phonograph records of sweet band music into a cone-shaped microphone at the radio studio of 8MK, the only commercial signal in Michigan (its call letters changed to WBL in October, then to WWJ the following year), the Mitchell Phonograph Company began manufacturing its own line of record players, and radio receivers at the northeast corner of Gratiot Avenue and Mitchell Street.[1]

Four years later, Mitchell Phonograph built a three-story factory with product showrooms right across Gratiot, and sold Mitchell labeled records.[2] Sporting a Detroit address, the discs were custom-made by the Bridgeport Die and Machine Company in Bridgeport, Connecticut, with music supplied by Paramount Records, based at the Wisconsin Chair Company of Port Washington, Wisconsin; and by the Emerson Phonograph Company, owned by the Scranton Button Company of Scranton, Pennsylvania.[3] (Around the same time, the J.L. Hudson department store of Detroit held a similar contract with Bridgeport D&M to make records with a Hudson brand label.)[4]

During the Roaring Twenties, Detroit boasted renowned groups with major label contracts, such as the celebrated jazz orchestra McKinney's Cotton Pickers,

---

1. "Mitchell Phonograph Company Celebrates Removal to New Home," *Detroit Free Press* (May 17, 1925. Vol. 90, No. 232), 13.

2. John Milan, *Detroit — Ragtime and the Jazz Age* (Charleston SC, Chicago IL, Portsmouth NH, San Francisco CA, 2009), 83.

3. "Paramount Records," https://en.wikipedia.org/wiki/Paramount_Records (Accessed 2021). "Paramount Records Basics," https://the78rpmrecordspins.wordpress.com/2013/02/28/paramount-record-basics/ (Accessed 2021). "Emerson Records," https://en.wikipedia.org/wiki/Emerson_Records (Accessed 2021)

4. "Equal All Ways," Zayde's Turntable, https://zaydesturntable.wordpress.com/tag/bridgeport-die-and-machine-company/ (Accessed 2021). Milan, op. cit., 70.

as well as Jean Goldkette's dance music outfits (these organizations recorded for the Victor label).

Perhaps because of the attention paid by major companies to Detroit musicians during the era, and a general scarcity of people with knowledge of recording technology, nary a Detroit-based record company materialized to exploit local talent. Another reason may have been the precipitous drop in record sales in 1927, coinciding with enormous numbers of new radio stations cropping up across the country.[5] Although these nascent signals offered thousands of musicians — professionals and amateurs alike — time to fill the airwaves with noise, a constant need for content led most broadcasters to rely, at least in part, on recorded music — a practice the record industry blamed for its sales decline.

And then the Great Depression arrived in 1929. Most of the record-buying public shifted attention to

---

5. Jack Sher, "Meet the Juke Box," *Detroit Free Press – Sunday Magazine* (June 23, 1940. Vol. 110, No. 50), 8.

acquiring jobs, food, shelter, and medicine. Major record labels recorded fewer artists, and issued fewer discs. Across the world, small record companies collapsed. The most successful independent American platter pushers, such as Paramount, and Gennett, ceased production (both closed, or sold their master recordings in 1935), or were gobbled up by larger concerns.

After American Prohibition ended in 1933, a new assortment of juke boxes — fancy wood cabinets filled with a stack of ten or twelve of the latest popular records available to hear at the drop of a nickel — flourished in arcades, soda shops, restaurants, beer gardens, hotel lounges, and social halls. Buying records during the Depression was a luxury for most people, and although a body had to leave one's home to experience it, this on-demand entertainment grew very popular.

By 1937, juke box operators purchased six out of ten of all records made in the U.S.A. Most of these businesses worked independently, placing and maintaining juke boxes in public spaces, with arrangements to share profits with venue proprietors, in their own neighborhoods, cities, and regions. For example, on the east side of Detroit, an ex-convict with some electrician skills established a route managing coin-operated games and juke boxes near the Chrysler, Hudson, and Continental Motors factories. In what proved to be a prescient move, this man sought out a slick-haired, semi-retired vaudeville entertainer to make recordings for him. Unfortunately, the slick-haired vaudevillian wouldn't live long enough to hold copies of his records in his own hands.

★ ★ ★
RENOWN
Mfg. By Renown Records, 11629 Linwood, Detroit, Mich.

5008-A
Trianon Publications
BMI

Unbreakable Under
Normal Use

HANDY MAN
(Shoun Bros.)

SHOUN BROTHERS
With
String Band Accompaniment

★ ★ ★
RENOWN
Mfg. By Renown Records, 11629 Linwood, Detroit, Mich.

5008 B
Trianon Publications
BMI

Unbreakable Under
Normal Use

GRIDDLE GREASING DADDY
(Lewis Starr)

JOHNNY BUCKETT
And His
Cumberland River Boys

1 | shoun brothers

During the community lockdowns of pandemic year 2020, I often wandered through a forest of oak, beech, and maple trees surrounding a branch of the Rouge River flowing past a 1960s house that I'd purchased in a "time capsule" state. While I renovated — resetting patio stones, installing new flooring, and building a new kitchen — a song played in my head, over and over. I imagined myself lowering the tonearm of a turntable to play a certain 78 rpm record I had stored away in a ten-inch square cardboard box during my move. "I'm a handy man to have around / I'd like to tell you, I'm a handy man," went the refrain, sung by, according to the black print of the record's bright yellow paper label, the Shoun Brothers.

It's a disc unknown to all but die-hard collectors of old hillbilly records. Manufactured by Jack Brown of Detroit-based Fortune Records during the decade after the end of World War II, an era regarded as a boom time for small, independent record companies, the disc presented "Handy Man," backed with Johnny Buckett's "Griddle Greasing Daddy," on Brown's little Renown label in 1951.[1] The disc appeared forty-some releases into

---

1. In the record's dead wax area near the label, the code "157-A" was mechanically stamped into the master, and scratched out. A handwritten "5008A" appears next to it. The B-side has only a hand-written "5008B." Fortune discographies don't identify a 157 in the label's catalog, suggesting Jack Brown originally planned to press "Handy Man" on Fortune. Brown also issued a 45 rpm version on purple paper with silver ink. Yet another pressing of the 45 substituted the Shoun Brothers with Buckett's version of Hank Penny's 1947 "Let Me Play With Your Poodle" (itself a remake of a 1942 record by Tampa Red).

Brown's catalog, which he started in 1946 as a means to promote pop songs written by his wife Devora.[2]

Numbered 5008, the record was preceded by "Shotgun Wedding" (5001), a comical bluegrass performance by Rufus Shoffner, and "She Won't Turn Over For Me" (5002), by Floyd Compton's country-western band with a vocal by guitarist Tommy Odom.[3] What happened to 5003 through 5007 is anyone's guess. Perhaps they were "party records" of off-color comedy, hawked by Brown surreptitiously from under his sales counter.

When they issued the Shoun Brothers disc, Brown and his wife devoted a good chunk of resources to courting a regional audience that spent sacks of nickels in juke boxes to hear country music. After just a few years in the business, the Browns found that records with ribald titles sold quite well.[4] For example, in 1950 they issued "Dirty Boogie," a swinging romp by Roy Hall and his Cohutta Mountain Boys, which was so successful they manufactured versions with two different B-sides.

Curiously, "Handy Man" sounded like country music of the late 1930s, rather than 1950, with standard steel guitar (pedals would turn popular a few years later), fiddle, rhythm guitar, and mandolin. "I'll paint

---

2. For the story on Jack and Devora Brown, and Fortune Records, see: Billy Miller and Michael Hurtt, *Mind Over Matter: The Myths and Mysteries of Detroit's Fortune Records* (New York: Kicks Books, 2020).

3. The label of Renown 5002 "She Won't Turn Over For Me" misspelled Odom's name as "Odim," and credited the song to Lewis Starr.

4. The history of raunchy commercial recordings reaches back to the age of audio cylinders made in the 1890s. Jody Rosen, "There Once Was a Record of Smut ..." *New York Times* (July 8, 2007) https://www.nytimes.com/2007/07/08/arts/music/08jody.html (Accessed 2021)

your porch, I'll fix your fire / You just relax, because I don't get tired / I'm a handy man to have around / I'd like to tell you, I'm a handy man" is as hokum as it gets. The audio playback from the record often distorts from the recording level having been set too high — a hallmark of many records that Jack Brown made at the studio he built in the back of his record shop on Third Street. However, this record was made before Brown moved his business to Third Street in 1956. The address on Renown 5008 is 11629 Linwood Street. Before he assembled his own recording space, Brown contracted local sound studios and engineers to record the artists featured on his labels.

Johnny Buckett was a pen name for Ernest Tubb soundalike John Thomas Chisenhall, a native of Clarksville, Tennessee. Born in 1926, he moved to Detroit in 1951. "Griddle Greasing Daddy" included Chisenhall's rhythm guitar, an electric guitar played in the style of Tubb's longtime guitarist Billy Byrd, standard steel guitar, and piano, with a melody borrowed from "Handy Man." The recording quality was finer than "Handy Man," yet the performance sounded stuck in the 1940s, instead of the driving honky tonk that country-western nightclub patrons preferred at the time. Chisenhall crooned verses such as, "I'd like to grease your griddle eight times or ten / Smoke a cigarette, and start all over again / I'm a griddle greasing daddy / I wanna grease your griddle until the break of dawn."

It was Chisenhall's first record, and Brown placed "Griddle Greasing Daddy" on the B-side of Renown 5008. Years later, Chisenhall revisited the song with a rock'n'roll beat. He also cut an album of religious music for Fortune. Brown pressed his last record, the novelty "Hippie In A Blunder," in 1967. Chisenhall died in Warren, Michigan, twenty years later.

The Shoun Brothers never appeared on records again — at least in name. When investigating Detroit's recorded history, I often asked local record collectors, "Who were the Shoun Brothers?" The resulting conversations usually turned to the York Brothers, George and Leslie — who made the Detroit juke box hit "Hamtramck Mama" — and whether the Shoun Brothers was an alias of theirs. After comparing voices, it didn't sound like the same boys to me. When I questioned musicians who played country music in Detroit during the 1940s and 1950s, "Did you ever run across an act called the Shoun Brothers?" — the answer was "No," every time. This pattern of inquiry went on for a couple of decades before I discovered the Shoun Brothers was an alias, after all.

Occasionally, I searched the Internet for the Shoun Brothers and found nothing new. A reference to an obscure duo who performed on radio and TV strictly around East Tennessee during the 1950s seemed promising. Based on the great numbers of people from the South who moved to Detroit for work, it could have been them. Perhaps they worked in a factory for a few weeks, before deciding to move on.

Results from an online search for the song title eventually pointed me to the answer. A group of young men posted a video of themselves performing "Handy Man" with the same instruments and arrangement as the old record. Among the viewer comments, a member of the band credited the Shelton Brothers, Bob and Joe, of

Texas. "I'm A Handy Man To Have Around" appeared on the flip side of the Shelton Brothers' 1941 country hit "Coo See Coo," issued by Decca Records. The Shoun Brothers on Renown is the same recording.[5] Well-known stars of the 1930s and 1940s, the Shelton Brothers made more than one hundred and fifty sides for Decca. Having little experience with country music before he started Fortune Records, how did Jack Brown come to release a bootleg of a popular act's ten-year-old hit? And where did the name Shoun Brothers come from?

Jack Brown referred to the name "Shoun" again, too. In 1961 he issued the first Fortune Records long-play album, "The Original Skeets McDonald's Tattooed Lady," a compilation of hillbilly party tunes, most of which debuted on Detroit juke boxes during the 1940s and 1950s. One of Fortune's best sellers, the album included three songs credited to "Shoun" — "Hamtramck Mama" and "Highland Park Girl," both originally recorded by the York Brothers, and "She Won't Turn Over For Me" performed by Tommy Odom. The Shoun name was my key to discovering that, unlike "Lewis Starr," a name that Brown reportedly invented to use whenever he needed a songwriter attribution to print on a record label, "Shoun" referred to a real person — a man who helped set the foundations for Detroit's home-grown record companies.

---

5. When I posted this observation on social media in March 2021, music writer Kevin Coffey responded that he came to the same conclusion twenty years before, and had spread the word among his network of Shelton Brothers and hillbilly music fans. Coffey's discovery didn't reach me, and my circle of record hounds.

2 | shades of an umbra

In 1792, blacksmith Leonard Shoun of Wythe County, Virginia, took his new bride, Barbara, across the Tennessee border into a picturesque, high valley.[1] One of the area's first white settlers, he called their Appalachian home Shouns Cross Roads. He forged iron into tools and equipment, and opened a public store.[2] By the end of Leonard's life, in 1845, he and his family owned many acres of land. Surrounded by the Iron Mountains to the north, Doe Mountain to the southwest, and Forge Mountain to the east, near the Tennessee-North Carolina border, several Shoun families had grown up in the area when the community changed its name to Mountain City, in 1885. In January 1894, four generations after Leonard, Charles Shoun, a farmer and laborer, and his wife Alice welcomed their first child (of ten) into the world. They named him Umbra Sylvester Shoun.

An "umbra" is defined as a shaded area, or the darkest zone of a shadow. This Umbra, whose stories are mostly unknown, is like a shadow to us. However, we can begin to understand him with a few details of his life: He was born with club foot. He grew up on a farm north of Mountain City, in Washington County, Virginia. At seventeen years old, he enlisted in the United States Army, serving in the Seventh Infantry Regiment, Company J, as a musician. Private U.S. Shoun's three-year tour ended

---

1. Joseph Pearce, "Note for: Leonard Shoun, 10 NOV 1771 - 9 JUN 1845," http://joepearce.com/gen/ghtout/np2.html (Accessed 2021)

2. Sh--n Family Association, "Leonard and Barbara's Family" (2006) https://shoun.net/f/shoun (Accessed 2021)

in 1914, after participating in the United States occupation of Vera Cruz, Mexico. A few months later, Shoun re-enlisted as a musician, serving with the Sixteenth Infantry Regiment, Company B — First Infantry Division, stationed at Fort Bliss near El Paso, Texas. His friends and family called him "Louie." He married (Madge), and engaged in the Mexican Expedition against Pancho Villa, under General John Joseph "Black Jack" Pershing. In 1917, he accompanied the American Expeditionary Force under General Pershing to France.

A grandson told me Shoun served as a personal aide to General Pershing. He returned from France at the end of 1917, with the rank of supply sergeant, a multi-pack per day cigarette habit (the U.S. Army included cigarettes in soldier rations), and tattoos on his arms and torso.

In January 1918, news reports appeared in East Tennessee, and Southeast Kentucky, about Sergeant U.S. Shoun giving public talks about the Sixteenth Infantry Regiment's first battle against German forces in France.[3] Reporters withheld the location, but it was probably near Bathelemont-les-Bauzemont in northeastern France.[4] In an effort to rally public interest in the war, and to sell United States bonds, Shoun told tales of trench warfare,

---

3. "Kentucky Boy Took German In His First Trip 'Over Top'," *Owensboro Messenger-Inquirer* (January 27, 1918), 8. "Experience of Soldier Over There," *Johnson City Staff* (February 13, 1918), 6. "'Over the Top' Pulaski County Boy's Experience In Capturing German Soldiers" *Lancaster Central Record* (February 21, 1918), 2. "Junction City," *Stanford Interior Journal* (February 22, 1918), 2.

4. Jake Sandlin, "Officer in WWI battled for state," *Arkansas Democrat Gazette* (April 9, 2017) https://www.arkansasonline.com/news/2017/apr/09/officer-in-wwi-battled-for-state-201704-1/ (Accessed 2021)

and going "over the top" to engage the enemy. German soldiers attacked American troops the night of November 3, 1917, first with artillery, then in hand-to-hand combat. Shoun told his audiences he captured a German soldier who refused to believe he was American, as the enemy weren't informed the U.S.A. had entered the war. "The barbarity of the Germans has not half been told," Shoun told his audiences. "I saw little children with arms, legs and ears cut off. This punishment was inflicted by the retreating Germans. They told me that babies were grabbed from their mothers' arms and a bayonet thrust through them …" Shoun also revealed "trench paralysis" caused him to convalesce for weeks at a military hospital, before he returned home. Nowadays we call it post-traumatic stress disorder. In June 1919, the French government awarded Shoun, and other American World War I veterans of French battlefields, the Croix de Guerre.

After he left the service, Shoun and his wife settled in Louisville, Kentucky, and raised two boys and a girl. Shoun worked for a taxi company, performing with the Yellow Cab Band until August of 1924, when he and the band's president joined a vaudeville orchestra.[5] He returned to the taxi garage six months later.[6] Although far from certain, Shoun's grandson suggested he played cornet, or trombone.[7] Shoun likely participated in army

---

5. "Taxi Band Honors Departing Officers," *Louisville Courier-Journal* (August 5, 1924. Vol. 140, No. 20,306), 16.

6. "Safety Buttons to be Given Out," *Louisville Courier-Journal* (January 4, 1925. Vol. 141, No. 20,458), 10.

7. Perhaps Shoun played cornet, and his nickname "Louie" originated in homage to the seminal jazz musician Louis Armstrong.

bands, such as the Sixteenth Infantry Band, which often performed in El Paso during the years he spent at Fort Bliss.

After his vaudeville adventure, Shoun divorced, and his ex moved with their children to New Mexico. Shoun joined his parents and several siblings in Detroit, and he worked as an auto repair mechanic on the east side of town. He soon began playing music in local dance bands. In 1928, Shoun married a divorcee (Mabel) and lived with her two daughters on Gratiot Avenue, between Forest and East Warren. Four years later, while living on the lower east side, the youngest girl died from respiratory diphtheria.

Along the line, he learned to repair radios and phonographs. In 1939, Shoun and family moved into an apartment attached to a storefront at 12942 East Jefferson Avenue, where he opened Universal Recording Studios, an audio transcription service.[8]

Shoun was a member of the Fairview post of Veterans of Foreign Wars (Fairview was an east side village annexed by Detroit in 1912), and joined the Freemasons. Eventually he opened Shoun Radio (and later Television) Service, just around the corner from Universal Recording Studios, at 965 Dickerson Avenue. But it was at Universal where he delivered the goods for which — after three quarters of a century in obscurity — we may celebrate his name.

---

8. In the 1940 Detroit City Census, Shoun's address was 12942 East Jefferson Avenue, his occupation "musician" in an "orchestra" (a term applied to most types of music ensembles during that era). On his 1942 draft registration card, Shoun stated he was self-employed at Universal Recording Studios.

Thomas Edward Kiely. *Illustration by Craig Muki*

3 | eddie the immune

On May 13, 1927, federal agents escorted a thirty-one year-old man from Detroit past fortified gates into the United States Penitentiary at Leavenworth, Kansas.[1] At five feet, seven inches tall, one hundred forty-eight pounds, and a clean-cut appearance — a boyish mug with mild expression topped by a full head of dark hair combed straight back — he seemed a person you wouldn't glance at twice, when passing on the street. His name was Thomas Edward Kiely, aka Ed Kiely, or "Eddie the Immune." Kiely's nickname referred to his record of more than eighteen arrests during the previous ten years, while he served time only once.

A week before, on May 6, Federal Judge Charles C. Simons sentenced Kiely to six years prison and a $2,000 fine for conspiring to and violating the Dyer Act, which prohibited the interstate transport of stolen cars. The brains behind a ring of thieves, Kiely was ratted out by partners Max Lipton, and Ben Feldman, who was based in Buffalo, New York. Police in Buffalo apprehended Feldman for selling hot cars to second-hand dealers. He and Lipton were sentenced to serve four and nine months, respectively, in the Detroit House of Corrections.[2]

---

1. National Archives at Kansas City. Record Group 129, Records of the Bureau of Prisons. Department of Justice, Bureau of Prisons. U.S. Penitentiary, Leavenworth. Inmate Case Files, 1895 – 1957. National Archives Identifier: 571125. Inmate # 27704.

2. "Notorious Motor Thief Sentenced," *Detroit Free Press* (May 7, 1927. Vol. 92, No. 222), 5.

Kiely was first arrested (for grand larceny) at age seventeen in Detroit, in 1914. In 1917, Kiely and two buddies attempted to extort a woman who ran a disorderly house.[3] Later that year, he teamed up with three others to rob a money collector for C.F. Smith grocery stores at gunpoint.[4] To avoid the slammer, Kiely joined the U.S. Army, serving in Ann Arbor, Michigan, where he attended vocational classes — most likely electrical training — at the University of Michigan, until his discharge in 1919.[5] He also tattooed his arms, chest, and back with American flags, bald eagles, a sailor, a serpent crawling out of a human skull, a woman in tights, Satan with bat wings, a pentagram, and the flag of Ireland.

Both of Kiely's parents immigrated from Ireland during the 19th century. Born in 1825, his father Thomas W. Kiely arrived in the U.S. in 1848. Three years later in Detroit, he married his first wife. Thomas W. worked as a railroad painter, laborer, and carpenter, settling downtown on Franklin Street, near railroad tracks that ran along the Detroit River. He built and renovated homes in the neighborhood, and purchased properties whose rentals grew his bank account. When he married his second wife, Margaret, he was sixty-six years old, and she was twenty-seven. I couldn't find much about her origins, although sources suggested she

---

3. "Alleged Blackmail Trio is Arrested," *Lansing State Journal* (January 18, 1917), 7.

4. "Two Are Arrested As Auto Bandits," *Detroit Free Press* (December 11, 1917. Vol. 88, No. 75), 12.

5. *Catalogue of the University of Michigan* (Ann Arbor: Published by the Universty, 1919), pp. 626, 643.

was an orphan. The union resulted in two children — Margaret arrived in 1893, and Thomas Edward in 1896 (just weeks before local inventor Charles Brady King took the first successful "horseless carriage" made in Detroit for a spin around downtown). By 1900, Thomas W. had retired from work.

At the dawn of the new century, Margaret took over management of her husband's real estate interests. In 1906, aged eighty-one years, Thomas W. died. His son was just ten years old. Kiely's mother held the family together, relying on her Catholic faith for inspiration. One can imagine her boy running wild in Detroit streets among horse-drawn wagons, early automobiles, trolleys, and trains that crossed nearby streets to reach riverfront railyards; and on foot: businessmen, factory workers, sharks and con-men, transitory railroad workers, and furloughed sailors who worked on the Great Lakes. When he wasn't in grade school or hauled into church by his mother, the old theater district on Monroe Street likely attracted Kiely for hours at a time.

Around 1919, Kiely's mother moved into a wood frame house at 121 South Lenox Avenue, north of Essex, in the Jefferson-Chalmers district, just a couple blocks away from an upscale development called Grayhaven. Edward Gray, at one time the head engineer of the Ford Motor Company's Highland Park plant, built Grayhaven on a marsh along the Detroit River by dredging a U-shaped canal and creating an island. Kiely and his mother must have observed the construction of many stately homes, including those of industrialist and motorboat pioneer Gar Wood, Lawrence Fisher, Arthur Buhl, William Koerber, and Harrington Walker.

A tenacious business dealer, Kiely's mother held enough property and means to influence police, finance lawyers, and pay fines to keep him out of jail. In 1923, she guaranteed her son's $10,000 bail, after his arrest for stealing a car (while awaiting trial, Kiely hired men to murder a key witness in the case against him — they failed, and were jailed). In January 1924, Judge Frank Murphy handed Kiely a sentence of three to ten years in Jackson State Prison. He was paroled in two. A year later, he was caught violating the Dyer Act and went to federal prison at Leavenworth. Inside the penitentiary, Kiely's technical aptitude, and — after a rocky start — willingness to follow the warden's rules helped him earn a good reputation among the staff. Eventually, he managed the electricity needs of the Leavenworth shoe factory, and even constructed a radio receiver with rooftop aerial antenna for the shop floor. He received an early release in 1931.

Kiely returned to Detroit to face the Great Depression, Prohibition, and Judge Murphy, who was elected mayor the previous year. He moved into his mother's house, and started a business by purchasing several coin-operated miniature bowling games and pinball machines, and placing them in east side beer gardens.

Kiely's mother, aged sixty-nine, died of heart failure in December 1934. A requiem high mass was sung in her honor at Saints Peter and Paul's Jesuit Church downtown, on East Jefferson Avenue, and Kiely and his sister laid her to rest in Mount Olivet Cemetery.[6] By then, the city had changed the numbering system of

---

6. "Obituaries," *Detroit Free Press* (December 24, 1934. Vol. 104, No. 234), 5.

its street addresses, which updated the house on Lenox Avenue to 519, where Kiely continued living. At some point during or before 1936, he dabbled in songwriting (*details to come, in chapter eight*).

In 1937, juke box manufacturers across America experienced an unprecedented boom. The application of new technologies by most companies led to more reliable performance, more selections (sixteen became standard — four more than in previous years), as well as a new eye-catching, streamlined aesthetic that included handmade art deco façades crafted with dazzling combinations of wood veneers, patterned fabrics woven with sparkling, metallic threads stretched over speakers, sculpted speaker grills, and colorful crystal lights that illuminated the machinery inside as it played customer selections — all of which improved their appeal, and popularity.

Kiely added a handful of these contraptions to his neighborhood route in the spring. A few months later, he enthused to a Detroit-based reporter for *Billboard*, a trade magazine covering the entertainment industry, that, compared to pinball machines, let alone bowling games, juke boxes were easy to place in small spaces, such as restaurants, and twenty-four-hour hamburger stands, where the machines drew plenty of coins, and continued to do so after neighborhood bars closed at two o'clock in the morning.[7]

In 2016, a grandson of Kiely's sister cheerfully told me his family claimed Ed Kiely as its "black sheep." He also admitted he wasn't aware of the stories you're about to read.

---

7. "Small Restaurants Use More Phonos," *Billboard* (November 27, 1937. Vol. 49, No. 48), 136.

4 | universal recording studios

On my shelf of records, two ten-inch wide shellac discs made in Detroit around 1940 sport labels that appear to be the same. With a second look though, I notice one reads "Universal" and the other "United." Upon even closer inspection, hand-written print along the bottom of one label states, "Universal Recording Studios — Detroit, Michigan." The other reads, "United Sound Systems ... Detroit, Mich." It's obvious the same person designed both labels, using the same graphic elements and a similar layout: the brands "Universal" and "United" scrawled by hand above the spindle holes; and above each brand, a badge with initials of the business contained inside a circle: "URS" and "USS." Design might have been the only connection between the entities behind these records — but maybe it wasn't.

What were these businesses? We might say, "record labels" — companies that hire musicians, record music, and release it for profit. These old companies did just that, but due to the eminent role juke boxes played as a means for the public to experience popular music, the business model differed in significant ways.

During the 1930s, making records required people with specialized knowledge working together through a complex process. A sound studio — often copied from radio station setups, including use of wall curtains and cork ceiling tiles — had to be specially prepared. Sound engineers placed microphones strategically near performers in one room, and used electronic controls in another room to manipulate up to three minutes of audio signals generated by microphones, sending the signals to a machine called a cutting lathe. The lathe used a tonearm-like apparatus with a special needle to etch grooves into a thick, smooth, waxy coating of a metal disc spun at a rate of seventy-eight revolutions per minute (the speed at which most commercial records spun on a record player). If the performance was good, and successfully transcribed, the etched disc was electroplated with a high-conductive metal, such as gold or silver, then set into another eighteen-hour electroplating bath to produce a copper plated "master" disc. The last step was repeated using the copper plated disc to make a duplicate. The master plate was stored in a safe place, and the copy used to create reversed impressions out of a metal alloy. These alloy plates, called "stampers," represented one side of a record. Once attached to a mechanical press, one stamper aligned above another, a press operator inserted paper labels by hand. A preheated "record biscuit," made of plastic ingredients, was pressed between the stampers, creating a flat record, usually ten, sometimes twelve inches wide, complete with audio grooves for turntable play.[1]

Outside of record production facilities, mostly owned by major labels, few people had direct knowledge of the process, and fewer could lay hands on the machinery. However, Detroit's industrial surge of the early 20th century gathered and cultivated the engineering

---

1. Jack Sher, "Of the Comeback of an Old, Old Friend: the Phonograph Record," *Detroit Free Press – Screen & Radio Weekly* (August 14, 1938. Vol. 108, No. 102), pp. 6-7. W. St.Clare Minturn, "Toscanini Makes Beethoven Fifth Symphony Record," *Decatur Daily Review* (March 9, 1940. Vol. 61, No. 161), 2. John Selby, "Music Via Waffle Irons, or How Records Are Made," *Fort Worth Star-Telegram* (May 18, 1941. Vol. 61, No. 107), 38.

knowledge and resources that helped a small group of enterprising folks build the technology to make modern recordings. James Siracuse, a musician with an extreme curiosity in the mechanics of recording, pioneered this trail in Detroit.

Born in French Tunisia to Italian parents in 1903, Siracuse arrived in the United States with his family in 1911. During the 1920s, Siracuse played violin in Detroit dance bands, while learning the tool and die trade. His brother Anthony repaired coin operated pianos for the W. W. Gunn Music House of Detroit. After the 1929 murder of Gunn Music owner William Wesley Gunn by thugs during an attempted kidnapping, Siracuse's brother rented the house next door to the family's digs in Dearborn, Michigan, in order to store and repair Gunn Music's juke boxes, and coin-operated instruments.[2]

Like his brother, Siracuse sold musical instruments and accessories during the late 1920s, through the 1930s. At his shop on Cass Avenue in Midtown, he experimented with making recordings, which could have attracted trade from local music publishing offices, such as the large Remick Corporation based downtown. However, Warner Bros. Music purchased Remick in 1929, and then the Great Depression arrived.

At a time when the few companies making cutting lathes demanded royalties from commercial productions, Siracuse built his own. Eventually, he figured out how to machine just about anything he required, and opened an audio transcription business where his services included

---

2. After the end of World War II, Anthony Siracuse started his own Circle Music juke box vending company in Detroit.

the new miracle of instant records, using lacquer coated discs whose surfaces could be engraved by a special lathe on the spot. In the mid-1930s, anyone could make a recording at Siracuse's studio, and walk out the door with a one-of-a-kind record the same day. Business managers could record advertisements to play over radio, songwriters could promote their works to publishers, musicians could make records to promote their acts, and private citizens could send personal audio greetings to family and friends anywhere in the world.

In 1939, Siracuse and his wife Esther expanded their operations into a large residential building with offices at 5840 Second Avenue, where they established the definitive iteration of "United Sound Systems." During World War II, Siracuse worked on films for the Army at the Paramount studio in Queens, New York.[3] After the war, he and his staff, including his brother Anthony, as well as his son, endeavored to perfect their studio spaces and equipment, earning a wide reputation for high quality recordings. From the 1940s through the 1970s, important musicians of local and national reputation, representing many popular genres, made recordings at United Sound, including Charlie Parker, Dizzy Gillespie, John Lee Hooker, Jackie Wilson, Johnnie Ray, Little Willie John, Jack Scott, Jimmy Work, Johnny Powers, Marv Johnson, Alberta Adams, George Clinton, and Johnnie Taylor. Meat-and-potatoes clients included local automakers,

---

3. Bob Olhsson, *Re: Marvin Gaye 'Here, My Dear' Information on Marvin's Room Studios, Reply #31* (ProSoundWeb online forum, Sept. 4, 2010) https://repforums.prosoundweb.com/index.php?topic=34139.30 (Accessed 2013)

advertising agencies, newspapers, radio broadcasters, television stations, movie makers, the Detroit Symphony Orchestra, Motown Records, and a variety of record companies, large and small.

After Siracuse sold the studio and retired in 1972, a series of new owners, notably Black musician-producer-banker Don Davis, kept United Sound Systems a going concern, making it America's oldest independent studio in continuous operation. In 2017, a Michigan Historical Marker was planted in a grassy patch in front of the building.[4] Siracuse died in 1988.

While reminiscing about working at United Sound Systems as a young man during the 1960s, Ed Wolfrum, a brilliant Detroit-bred audio engineer and inventor, said that Siracuse, from his earliest endeavors, helped establish and promote other recording studios in Detroit.[5] While he strove to manage the finest audio facilities around, Siracuse believed friendly competition would increase business for the field overall. One of his earliest collaborations must have been Universal Recording Studios. How did he meet Louie Shoun? Perhaps they played music together in local dance bands. I may be wrong, but without help from a man such as Siracuse, how else could Shoun open his own transcription service in 1939? Why does United Sound Systems share Umbra S. Shoun's initials? Why do the labels on my two 78s sport the same design? Wouldn't unfriendly firms object to such a situation?

---

4. To view the historical marker online, visit the Detroit Sound Conservancy at https://detroitsound.org/unitedsound/ (Accessed 2022)

5. Miller and Hurtt, op. cit., 2-3.

A view of the lower east side business district on East Jefferson Avenue, facing east from Gray Street, photographed in 1940. At right, Universal Recording Studios was tucked into the next block over. The home of the Universal/Mellow Record Company and Shoun's radio repair service was

around the first corner east of the studio, on Dickerson Avenue. On the north side of East Jefferson, Ed Kiely opened what became the main Mellow Music Shop in the block beyond the Hotel Savarine.
Image source: Detroit Historical Society, all rights reserved

Harry G. Graham. *Illustration by Craig Maki*

5 | marquette music company

Although he pressed records with United Sound labels, Siracuse never sought to compete in the record making business. Discs made by United Sound were custom productions pressed in small quantities. Universal's story diverged from Siracuse's model of how a recording service functioned, by evolving into the first Detroit studio linked to a record company. Most likely, no one saw this development coming, not even Louie Shoun.

Political and military aggressions in Europe and Asia during the 1930s worried American leaders, and debates about the country's isolationist stance led some to propose turning industry's attentions to supporting our allies around the world, as well as increasing material reserves to defend the nation's territories. As the American manufacturing sector expanded, after its lowest point in 1933, thousands of people from the South moved to Detroit for work. White Southerners filled rentals as soon as they became available in neighborhoods surrounding Chrysler's east side factory, among a plethora of machinery makers, and suppliers. Nightclubs and restaurants along East Jefferson Avenue pulled in good business from these workers.

East of the large factories, in a vibrant shopping district of eateries, five-and-dime stores, doctor offices, hardware stores, gas stations, clothiers, grocers, hotels, and a small theater, Shoun operated Universal Recording Studios. One of his first customers was Harry G. Graham, general manager of the Marquette Music Company, and the head of its new record sales and distribution arm: Wolverine Music and Specialties Company.

The largest vending machine business in Detroit, as well as the state of Michigan, Marquette Music was four decades old. Originator John A. Marquette (1877–1941) grew up in Detroit, eventually managing restaurants, and building coin-operated player pianos that he installed in saloons, hotels, and restaurants, at the turn of the century. As amusement machines evolved, his company ventured into games, and slot machines. In 1920, Marquette owned the Marquette Cafe at Woodward and McNichols, and he opened a real estate office. Although he and his family settled down in Marine City, his place of birth, Marquette's main business, and his social life, including a membership in the Detroit Yacht Club, stayed anchored in Detroit.[1] Marquette retired during the mid-1930s, when his company finished replacing its coin-operated pianos with the newest generation of juke boxes.

Marquette Music stayed out front of competitors in the region by deploying thousands of machines. It helped that, while working at Marquette Music for more than a decade, Harry Graham, aka "Mr. Music in Detroit" among the trade, represented the Michigan territory for the Rudolph Wurlitzer Company's brand of juke boxes. In September 1939, he opened Wolverine Music in Detroit.[2] Just a few weeks later, Graham approved payment of a $300 fee to record the York Broth-

---

1. "Retired Cafe Owner Dies," *Port Huron Times Herald* (February 13, 1941), 24.

2. Graham also managed Wolverine Music satellite offices in Cleveland and Cincinatti, Ohio. "Hearings Before the Special Committee

ers, an undistinguished hillbilly duo from Kentucky who had been playing Detroit's east side taverns regularly for about a year.

In May 1940, *Billboard* magazine printed Graham's explanation of how he chose the York Brothers: "We like to pick a band or artist nobody knows. Those with something of a name are too expensive and usually are under contract to one of the big recording companies."[3] Graham knew that records of different musical styles sold well in different neighborhoods. Along the industrialized sections of the east side, country-western discs attracted plays in many places catering to adults. Graham may have heard about Leslie York's "Hamtramck Mama," one of the songs the York Brothers recorded for him, from the proprietor of a tavern where the York Brothers performed regularly, such as the Kentucky Pool Hall on Harper Avenue near Helen Street. Said proprietor might have expressed interest in placing a record of the song in the juke box of his bar. Despite the short time they'd lived in Detroit, the York Brothers may have developed a reputation that Graham, who claimed he was his own talent scout, couldn't ignore.

In 1939, the average juke box earned fifteen to twenty dollars in coins every week, while just eight dollars was required to break even.[4] With sixteen to twenty records in every juke box (depending on the model), operators

---

to Investigate Organized Crime in Interstate Commerce," United States Senate, Eighty-Second Congress. First Session, Pursuant to S. Res. 202. Part 9, Michigan (February 8, 9, and 19, 1951), 969 – 974.

3. "Making of Local Records Has Points Pro and Con," *Billboard* (June 1, 1940. Vol. 52, No. 22), 78.

4. Sher, "Meet the Juke Box," op. cit.

rotated five or six new records into machines weekly. The operator counted plays to see what records won over patrons, and replaced any discs that had been engaged more than eighty-five times, or displayed signs of damage, such as scratches, chips, or cracks.[5] Some net profits (generally, less than half) were shared with owners of the spaces where operators placed their juke boxes, which kept most proprietors interested in their musical contents.

Graham's "private label" record-making venture broke new ground, and not only in Detroit. Juke box operators of North America took note when *Billboard* reported "One record scored solidly with operators"[6] — which could only have meant "Hamtramck Mama" — increasing sales by fifteen percent during its first six months on the market.

In November 1939, *Billboard* published a photo of Graham surrounded by jovial Wurlitzer representatives, and a few Detroit juke box operators, with their arms around each other. At the far right of the picture sat Ed Kiely, leaning away from the others as if to avoid being in the shot, grinning sheepishly at the camera.[7]

---

5. Records damaged more easily than those made after World War II, when record manufacturers introduced new plastic materials and formulas that improved durability, and audio reproduction.

6. "Making of Local Records Has Points Pro and Con," op. cit. *Billboard*'s policy against the mention of risqué novelty titles left it to the reader to decipher the subject of discussion was "Hamtramck Mama." Historical evidence — the numbers of surviving copies of the disc — supports this premise.

7. This item, and an earlier blurb ("Amusement Machines (Music)," *Billboard* (Sept. 2, 1939. Vol. 51, No. 35), 73.), suggest Wurlitzer was among the brands, or the brand, of Kiely's juke boxes. "Amusement Machines (Music)," *Billboard* (Nov. 11, 1939. Vol. 51, No. 45), 69.

6 | york brothers

After attending school through eighth grade, George York spent most of the 1920s working in the mines of Eastern Kentucky, before moving to Denver, Colorado, where he sang with a group on radio stations. By 1936, he'd come back east, settled in Jasper, Ohio, and married. He also began performing at the new WPAY[1] radio station, south of Jasper in Portsmouth, on the Ohio River.

As youngsters, George (born 1910) and his brother Leslie (born 1917) performed in a family string band for church, and social events in their hometown of Louisa, Kentucky. When George lived in Denver, Les joined the Civilian Conservation Corps in Kentucky, continued playing music, and won a radio contest in Lexington. Not long after George got on WPAY, Les joined him, and they promoted themselves as the York Brothers.

Mere months into their musical partnership, the Ohio River's devastating floods of January 1937 threw a wrench into the works. George and his wife fled to Colorado, where their son was born a few months later. Les and his wife ventured up U.S. Route 23, the famous "Hillbilly Highway," seeking work in the auto factories of Detroit. By 1939, George and Les had moved their families and guitars to Detroit's east side. They resumed their musical partnership at night, playing in neighborhood taverns, often for audiences of workers from the South, after laboring themselves in factories during the day.

---

1. WPAY radio was sometimes referred to as "Pay Any Yodeler," in reference to its country music programs, and the influence of Jimmie Rodgers, the popular "blue yodeler" who died in 1933.

Due to an old injury to his left thumb, George played rhythm guitar with a unique approach, combining single note runs accented by open chords in an old-time style suited for accompanying fiddle, or other popular stringed instruments. Les played lead guitar, some steel guitar, and mandolin, with licks flavored by traditional Appalachian songs, blues, and popular tunes. Having learned fundamentals of public performance from friends and relatives schooled in methods of the previous century, George and Les plucked the strings of their acoustic instruments for volume, and projected their voices. Although the York Brothers sometimes invited other musicians, such as fiddlers, bassists, and steel guitarists to join them on stage, when they entered Universal Recording Studios toward the end of 1939, it was just the two of them, with their guitars.

Les York brought to the session an uptempo blues inspired by the wide-open reputation of Hamtramck, a suburb dominated by the Dodge Main Plant, and incorporated in 1922 to prevent annexation by Detroit. During Prohibition, and for years after its demise, Hamtramck was known as a hornet's nest of people seeking illicit booze parties, gambling, blind pigs, and cathouses. "Hamtramck Mama" (Universal 105) featured lyrics such as, "You can tell her not to do it, but she'll do it just the same / She's a Hamtramck mama that no man can tame." Comparable in melody to the old "Deep Elem Blues" (which the Shelton Brothers revived during the 1930s), verses of "Hamtramck Mama" also mentioned impotent lawmen and corruptible preachers.

For the other side of the record, the York Brothers waxed "Little White Washed Chimney," a popular folk song they retitled "Going Home" (Universal 106). In this version, a notable change to the common lyrics made reference to the lives of many Detroit workers, for instead of singing "I went a-way up north, where money I would find ..." the Yorks sang, "Well, they told me to go to Detroit, where money I would find hangin' like apples on a tree / It was like my sweetheart told me, there was nothing of the kind. And the weather was so cold, I thought I'd freeze / So I'm going back ..."

Featuring regional connections that touched on universal themes, the tunes were chosen to appeal to a local audience. One song made light of vice in the big city, and the other described the plight of homesick workers.

Harry Graham placed an initial order of two thousand records pressed with Universal labels that featured "Distributed by Marquette Music Co. / Detroit" printed on them. Within weeks, Graham ordered a second pressing of five thousand, after juke box operators swept up copies of the first run. Demand for the record spread quickly across Detroit, and Graham began selling it to operators in Ohio, and Illinois, besides Michigan.[2]

In April 1940, the *Detroit Free Press* revealed Hamtramck council members and Mayor Walter Kanar had declared a ban on "Hamtramck Mama" within the city, urging Detroit officials to do the same.[3] The story appeared in newspapers, and on radio programs across

---

2. "Making of Local Records Has Points Pro and Con," op. cit.

3. After an investigation into corruption, Mayor Kanar was ousted from his position a couple of years later. "'Hamtramck Mama' Getting the Deaf Ear," *Detroit Free Press* (April 20, 1940. Vol. 109, No. 352), 1. "Smutty Disk Gets City Fathers' Ire," *Billboard* (May 4, 1940. Vol. 52, No. 18), 76.

the country[4] — resulting in even more sales. The *Detroit Times* reported Grinnell Brothers music store "would like to solve the mystery of who recorded 'Hamtramck Mama' for which they have had more calls and more requests in the past two weeks than any waxing in weeks. There is no point in calling, however, for none of our leading record counters have it."[5] At first, the disc was sold only to juke box operators. Although, one could find copies from second-hand record dealers, to whom juke box operators sold their used discs. Within a year or two, new copies could be purchased in smaller music shops around town.

The notoriety may have played a role in Les York receiving a layoff notice at his day job. He resettled in Portsmouth, Ohio, where, a few weeks later, he heard syndicated NBC radio newsman Lowell Thomas discuss "Hamtramck Mama," and the outcry by Detroit community leaders against it.[6] At twenty-two years old, Les was suddenly famous for a song hated by the most powerful men in Detroit. Fearing he'd done something illegal, he decided not to go back.

---

4. Even syndicated column "Scene on Broadway" brought up the song's title: "Several leading coin phonograph promoters have approached song writers in an attempt to have them compose songs about various localities around the country. ... Along came a song writer and turned out a tune called 'Hamtramck Mama' ..." Justin Gilbert, "Circling the Square," *Bergen Evening Record* (April 22, 1940. Vol. 45, No. 274), 22.

5. "Clinton Is Tops With 10-Mile Hop," *Detroit Times* (April 28, 1940), 103.

6. Despite the year printed in this source, the historical record shows most of the ruckus regarding "Hamtramck Mama'" occurred in 1940. "Back in 1939 a song entitled 'Hamtramck Mama' hit nation's headlines. Lowell Thomas used 30 minutes talking about it." "Notes To You-All," *Nashville Tennessean* (January 7, 1947. Vol. 40, No. 238), 3.

YORK BROTHERS

7 | hamtramck mama

Six years later, after the York Brothers each received service discharges from the United States Navy, they began making records in Nashville, Tennessee, for the Bullet label, a record company that helped incubate the music industry that developed Nashville into "Music City." Owner Jim Bulleit contracted several acts appearing on WSM radio, and its Saturday night "Grand Ole Opry," whose cast included the York Brothers. Their third record for Bullet presented a new version of "Hamtramck Mama." An ad for the disc in the December 30 edition of the *Nashville Banner* exclaimed, "Over 300,000 Copies Sold in Detroit Alone!!"[1]

In mid-1940, George York convinced his brother to return to Detroit by pointing out the attention "Hamtramck Mama" drew from all over the country was selling thousands of records, and resulted in offers of lucrative bookings for the York Brothers.

Marquette Music's pressings of "Hamtramck Mama" circulated for months, before a third version of the labels appeared. Black ink on red paper stated: "Manufactured by Universal Record Co. / 12942 E. Jefferson – Detroit."

As Graham's record enterprise exceeded expectations, Marquette Music exited the field. After Graham explained his strategy to *Billboard* magazine that spring, Detroit operator unions published warnings against placing "smutty" records in their machines. In December, juke box

---

1. "Hamtramck Mama" on Bullet was the third and last version of the song waxed by the York Brothers. Advertisement for Bullet Records, *Nashville Banner* (December 31, 1946. Vol. 40, No. 232), 11.

makers sent a similar message.[2] Such declarations had appeared in previous years, but the timing of these must have turned up some heat on Graham. He cooled his tail by removing references to Marquette Music from subsequent records. Without Graham, or possibly with his secret support, Shoun continued exploring the path "Hamtramck Mama" had blazed.

The war's disruptions to manufacturing forced Wurlitzer to pause production in 1942. Besides records, Graham began distributing beer, and hustled horse racing bets on the side. In June 1944, Detroit police raided Wolverine and arrested an employee found running a betting racket.[3] Some months later, a group of men, including Angelo Meli of Detroit's Italian mafia, convinced Graham to transfer his Wurlitzer account to them. This act, a mafia push for control of Detroit's vending businesses, pushed Graham into management of a bar at 501 East Jefferson, a few blocks away from his former office. He returned to sales in 1947, though — first in Indianapolis, Indiana, pushing Aireon juke boxes, then in Detroit, where he bounced around different companies through the mid-1950s.

Harry DeSchryver, an in-law of John Marquette, owned Marquette Music, and after Graham's departure, he and his nephew Vic DeSchryver eventually sold off Wolverine (which also marketed Aireon juke boxes after the war). In 1946, Vic took over Marquette Music. In 1958, he left the business for good.

---

2. "Phono Manufacturers in New Move Against Smut," *Billboard* (December 28, 1940. Vol. 52, No. 52), 133. "Detroiters Hit Naughty Disks," *Billboard* (August 3, 1940. Vol. 52, No. 31), 70.

3. "On Doorstep," *Detroit Free Press* (June 15, 1944. Vol. 114, No. 42), 1.

Graham had told *Billboard* in 1940 he was considering producing more local records, and a Marquette Music promotion appeared on (at least) one other disc — a sentimental pop record via United Sound Systems (*see the label reproduced on p. 22* [4]) — besides "Hamtramck Mama." However, no other disc with ties to Marquette Music is as well-known today. Shoun and the York Brothers followed up their success with another party record for the ages.

With more titles celebrating local environs, the second record by the Yorks — "Detroit Hulu Girl" (Universal 108) and "Highland Park Girl" (Universal 107) — presented not one, but two tales of raunchy romance, performed with a hot, swinging steel guitar. The lyrics of "Detroit Hulu Girl" described a lady friend who enjoyed partying to Hawaiian music — a genre that was trending popular. Performed with a quick tempo, the steel guitar screamed like a banshee as George and Les picked percussive licks behind it, crooning sweet brotherly harmonies that soared over the maelstrom of music behind their voices.

The flip side, "Highland Park Girl," was named after the incorporated factory town (dominated by Ford Motor Company) that, like Hamtramck, Detroit eventually surrounded. George, in waggish manner, warbled a humorous narrative about a man who came to realize he was dating a married woman only when he met her

---

4. Again, note the similarities of the labels on p. 22, then consider: United's early custom pressings mainly included jazz, pop, and skating rink organ music, amounting to a catalog of the era's most popular music styles. In contrast, the Universal catalog included sounds out of the mainstream (e.g., a German band, local choirs, a college glee club, and hillbilly music) as well as novelty/risqué songs.

husband, and his flying fists. Shoun pressed the record with blue paper and silver ink labels that gave them a similar appearance to early "Hamtramck Mama" records, except he specified: "Manufactured by Universal Record Co." with his East Jefferson address.

Although this record's sales amounted to more than you could shake a stick at, "Hamtramck Mama," the York Brothers' defining moment in Detroit, overshadowed all of those that came after. The unlikely hit, fabricated during the jazzy swing era, featured verses just clean enough for pundits to feel safe writing about in newspapers, and magazines. Although the press generally ignored the off-color records (and other types of music) that Shoun — and soon Ed Kiely —

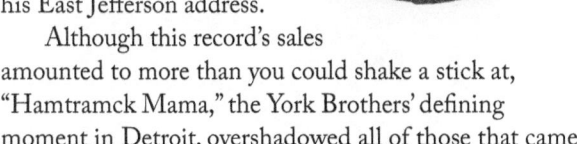

produced, the proverbial horse was out of the Universal Recording Studios barn. Orders from record buyers "in-the-know" kept the barn doors open for business, even as the music on the records changed.

Earl Gilson. *Illustration by Craig Maki*

8 | never be forgotten

Despite the coin machine conquests of the York Brothers, Louie Shoun didn't limit himself to recording country music. The first Universal record featured the Heidelberg Eight, a "German dance band" composed of horns, clarinets, and drums. They broadcast on WEXL radio Royal Oak, from 1935 through 1940. In 1939, they launched Universal with a polka titled "Toward The Stream" (Universal 101), backed with "The Leader" (Universal 102), a waltz. The labels (*one of which is reproduced on page 22*) presented the names of all participants: eight men, plus a leader. As a custom order, the studio's street address wasn't included.

"Hamtramck Mama" must have raised Universal's profile, whether people regarded the famous record in good or bad taste. When Harry Graham retreated from making records, Shoun's neighbor Ed Kiely entered the picture, seized the reigns, and finished blazing a trail. His fingerprints are all over productions that followed the York Brothers' first discs. When Kiely told Shoun his ideas for new Universal records, he brought two recordings in hand, both made during, or before, 1936.[1]

One record presents evidence Kiely had a creative interest in music. He collaborated with a man named Bernie Rose on lyrics for "Please, Mr. President!" (Universal 111), described on the label as a "Patriotic

---

1. I wonder: Because he had recordings prepared for manufacture, Ed Kiely might have already devised a plan to make records to sell to the juke box trade before Graham.

Dance March," and written in support of an American isolationist trend toward the surging political conflicts of Asia and Europe.[2] The song, as well as "My Dream" (Universal 115), were performed by vocalist Earl Gilson. Kiely coupled Gilson's recordings on two new discs produced with Universal labels, but with Kiely's home address (519 Lenox Ave.) under the words "Manufactured by Universal Record Co."

Gilson was born within sight of Lake Erie, in Port Clinton, Ohio, in 1892. He left behind his father's draying business in 1913 to begin a lengthy career in vaudeville

---

2. Another piece of evidence for Kiely's musical interests, and connections, appeared in Leavenworth prison files, which revealed in 1929 he wrote a letter to a woman in care of the Palace Theater (which, unknown to Kiely, had just closed its doors) on Monroe Street in Detroit. National Archives at Kansas City, op. cit.

— first, with a vocal quartette in Kansas City, Missouri. In 1915 he married, organized the Senate Trio (Gilson, W.J. "Billie" Brown, and Howard Bolinger), and toured the country. With a mane of slicked back, black "shoe polished" hair, and a wardrobe of dark tuxedos that refined his striking stage presence, Gilson went solo in 1918. In 1922-25, Gilson and his wife lived in Europe, where he headlined at theaters in London, and Paris as "America's Foremost Singing Conductor," before returning to his wife's hometown of Duluth, Minnesota. By 1928, he was back on the road, performing with Jack W. Scott in a duo known as the Radio Aces, in Michigan, and northern Ohio. In 1930, Gilson headlined a show on WMBC radio Detroit, where he met his second wife. They settled in the Nardin Park neighborhood, had a son, and Gilson made ends meet by selling products made by blind workers.

Now, here's the import of 1936 to Kiely's and Gilson's stories: In August of that year, at age forty-four Gilson died of cancer at the hospital in Ann Arbor, Michigan. His wife buried him in Grand Lawn Cemetery, on the west side.[3]

Gilson reportedly hustled for the song and sheet music publisher Jerome H. Remick — work in which the recordings that Kiely brought to Shoun might have originated.[4] The audio quality of Gilson's performances sound antiquated compared to Shoun's productions. The music seemed old-fashioned in 1940, as the beat did not

---

3. "Funeral of Earl Gilson Friday," *Fremont Messenger* (August 27, 1936), 2.

4. "Yester Years – Ten Years Ago Today," *Fremont Messenger* (May 4, 1936), 4.

Jack Campbell. *Illustration by Craig Maki*

"swing" the way of contemporary pop music. "Dance March?" How would you even move to that?[5]

Kiely may not have given Gilson's cuts as much consideration as we, because they wound up as flip sides to new recordings. "Please, Mr. President!" appeared with "You'll Never Be Forgotten" (Universal 112), a "Vocal / Ballad" by Jack Campbell. Campbell led bands in Detroit, including at the Graystone Ballroom during the first half of 1939, and then at Club San Diego. Born in Ireland in 1909, Campbell's family moved to West Palm Beach, Florida, in 1915. Ten years later, he worked nightclubs as a featured vocalist, and on radio. He appeared with the Johnny Hamp, and Vincent Lopez orchestras through the 1930s, and booked solo gigs on the side. In 1939 he and his Graystone Ballroom orchestra broadcast over WXYZ radio Detroit.[6]

After the U.S. entered World War II, Campbell traded Detroit for West Palm Beach. He married, joined a barbershop quartet, started a family, and sold insurance. Within a decade, he ran his own agency in Sarasota, where he died of a heart attack in 1958, aged forty-nine years.

---

5. Paul Gifford, archivist (retired) for the University of Michigan-Flint, answered my question of how people moved to dance marches: "The two-step got popular in 1891, danced to one of John Phillip Sousa's marches ["Washington Post March"], in 6/8 meter. ... By 1940 or 1950, at small-town dances some fiddlers might play an 'old-fashioned' two-step in 6/8. Later two-steps were danced to tunes such as 'Red Wing,' or ragtime. Then the fox trot came in around 1912, and lasted a long time." The two-step dance described is not to be confused with the circle two-step, or the Texas two-step. Gifford sent his explanation to the author via electronic message on October 31, 2021.

6. According to ads in the *Detroit Free Press*, Campbell led the house band at Detroit's Graystone Ballroom from January to April 1939.

Again, Bernie Rose appeared on the record label, as writer of "You'll Never Be Forgotten." The only Michigan reference to a Bernie Rose I could dig up was a member of the Marine City Lions Club who sang for and managed musical entertainment at club social events during the 1940s and 1950s. This Rose worked as an undertaker at a Marine City mortuary, where perhaps he spun a copy of "You'll Never Be Forgotten" over the funeral home's personal address system to comfort grieving families.

For those who banished grief by frequenting beer gardens, Kiely chose a torrid jazz number, "She Won't Turn Over For Me" (Universal 114) by Chick Fowler's Band,[7] to ride the back of Gilson's sentimental "My Dream." The unidentified musicians set a frantic pace (whipping up a fury untouched until their children and grandchildren created surf music and punk rock) with which vocalist Chick Fowler had trouble keeping up. This was just the beginning: "Johnny Jones bought a car just the other day / Took his girl out for a ride; thought that she would play / But he ran into trouble. Along the road they sit / And as you pass them by, you'll hear poor Johnny cry / Oooh, I can't get her started. I can't get her started. She won't turn over for me … Now her lines are all right, and her body's a sport / She won't do much on a gallon, but she'll raise hell on a quart …"

---

7. In January 1941, a "Ralph Lew Fowler" joined the American Federation of Musicians Detroit Local No. 5. In January 1943, "Ralph Lew (Chick) Fowler" was expelled from same local. A Ralph L. Fowler lived in an apartment on Cass Avenue, but this man signed his midde name "Lin" on his draft card. "Local Reports," *The International Musician* (January 1941. Vol. 39, No. 7), 34. "Suspensions, Expulsions, Reinstatements," *The International Musician* (January 1943. Vol. 41, No. 7), 24.

Despite a commendable effort in its assault on good taste, the record didn't touch "Hamtramck Mama" sales. But a decade later, guitarist Tommy Odom revived it, delivering a honky tonk version with Floyd Compton and his Western Troubadours on the Fortune Records subsidiary label, Renown.

Odom's knowledge of the number might have come from Detroit jazz guitarist Bob Mitchell, whose method sounded much like that performed on the Universal record (along with a pianist who played like Bobby Stevenson, Mitchell's friend and partner in music for many years. I'd hazard Chick Fowler's Band included an early quintet the young Stevenson led in Detroit before he joined the army — Perhaps the horn was blown by Louie Shoun, himself).

Born in Paris, Tennessee, in 1927, Odom arrived in Detroit in 1941. He told me Mitchell was his musical mentor, and friend.[8] The lessons made an impact, because Odom earned a reputation as one of the city's finest country-western guitar pickers, playing in local taverns through the 1990s. But when I asked him about Floyd Compton, and his fifty-year-old recording, Odom couldn't remember jack.

---

8. Craig Maki and Keith Cady interviewed Tommy Odom (1923-2010) on July 2, 2001.

9 | have a little talk

The next two Universal discs appeared without an address on the labels. The Bethany Chorus of the Ebenezer African Methodist Episcopal (AME) Church commissioned four recordings, pressing copies for members of the church, their friends, and families. It's likely Shoun and Kiely were in the process of setting up a new space for selling records, in a storefront shared by Shoun's radio repair shop, around the corner from the studio, on Dickerson Avenue. Considering the many missing catalog numbers in Universal's masters list (*see Discographies*), not every recording session led to the manufacture of commercial records. Unfortunately, these particular Universal discs are the only known recordings of African American artists on labels associated with Shoun.

In 1940, Reverend George W. Baber led the congregation of the Ebenezer AME Church at Willis and Brush streets. Odella Robinson presided over the Bethany Chorus, and Elizabeth Gary played the church organ and directed the music.[1] The recordings, a combination of nineteenth century jubilee singing and modern choir, presented with piano accompaniment, and *a capella*, exhibited brilliant — passionate, inviting — celebrations of faith.

Gary played "just about every instrument they made," said a son, William Gary. Born in South Carolina, she and her husband moved to Detroit during World War I. She also enjoyed jazz at the Graystone Ballroom, taught

---

1. "Schedules of Churches," *Detroit Tribune* (October 17, 1942. Vol. 20, No. 31), 14.

HAVE A LITTLE TALK

at the Detroit Community School of Music, composed, and imparted her love of music to young students, who included Mayor Coleman A. Young, jazz guitarist Kenny Burrell, and opera singer George Shirley, in the segregated Black Bottom neighborhood east of downtown.[2]

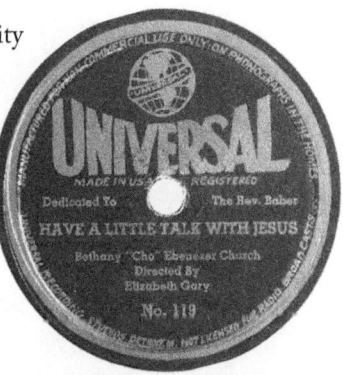

These joyous performances — possibly the first records documenting Detroit's rich African American traditions of religious music — were matched with an updated record label that included a bold new Universal title across the top, and North and South American continents depicted on a globe with a ribbon that read "Universal" stretched across it. The labels credited "Bethany 'Cho' Ebenezer Church / Directed By Elisabeth[sp.] Gary," and noted the vocalists. The label of "Have A Little Talk With Jesus" (Universal 119), featuring the full chorus, added a dedication to Rev. Baber. He was made a bishop in 1944, and died in 1970.

Gary participated in recordings through the years. The heading of a notice upon her death at eighty years old, in 1980, anointed Gary "a musical legend to Detroiters."[3]

---

2. Patricia Montemurri, "Elizabeth Gary a musical legend to Detroiters," *Detroit Free Press* (October 12, 1980. Vol. 150, No. 161), 5.

3. Ibid.

10 | it tain't no good

On September 16, 1940, President Franklin Delano Roosevelt signed a bill authorizing the first peacetime conscription in American history. One month later, sixteen-and-a-half million men registered with local draft boards, just in the state of Michigan. Although the president encouraged men to enlist voluntarily, there was a very real chance that any man eighteen to thirty-five years old would soon be called up, leaving families and jobs for a year of military training.

With U.S. participation in global hostilities looking more and more likely, the York Brothers attempted to dodge the approaching gloom with their next record. "Conscription Blues" (Universal 126) promoted mirth in a new, uncertain predicament that even the York Brothers found themselves in. The song began with a line performed with a yodel: "Uncle Sa-hamm is ca-hawl-lin' me-hee." Les picked guitar licks as if to set his strings on fire, and George shouted, "Yeah, boy! Got the conscription blues!" With exasperated resignation, the Yorks sang, "I don't know why they have to do these funny things to me / Although I know I'm living in a land of liberty / They made me sign with Uncle Sam — I guess they got you too … My baby said the other day that I just couldn't go / I said, 'Go speak to Uncle Sam,' but Uncle Sam said, 'No!' / They picked my number from the bowl, and sent the questionnaire / I guess there's nothing I can do, I'm hooked for just one year." It was as clever a song about moving from civilian to military life as was ever written.

Ed Kiely paired "Conscription Blues" with "Gamblers Blues" (Universal 402), in which the York Brothers re-used the melody of "Hamtramck Mama." The lyrics — narrated by a character whose notion of a good time involved gambling, drinking whisky, and chasing women — and the addition of a steel guitarist gave the song its own appeal. Displaying a new address, the record labels read, "Manufactured by Universal Record Company, 965 Dickerson, Detroit."

As a song writer, Les York reached beyond the risqué formula so profitable during the previous year. However, the York Brothers did cut a couple more: "That Nagging Young Husey[sp.]" (Universal 127), a waltz describing a young man's henpecked marriage, and "It Tain't No Good" (Universal 405), a blues about an over-the-hill floozy. They also waxed a melodramatic ballad, titled "Sweetheart Darling" (Universal 404), a sad lament about a recently deceased fiancé. Of these numbers, "It Tain't No Good," was issued two more times.[1] It must have been the best seller of the bunch.

During the winter of 1940-41, the York Brothers signed an agreement with major label Decca Records, and they stopped recording for Universal. In February, the Yorks traveled to Chicago, and cut six sides, including remakes of "Sweetheart Darling" (Decca 5933) and "That Nagging Young Husey" (Decca 5943), retitled "Speak To Me, Little Darling" and "Nagging Young Woman," respectively.

---

1. The melody of the York Brothers' "It Tain't No Good" retreads that of the Shelton Brothers' "I'm A Handy Man To Have Around."

The Decca recordings included heart songs with handles such as, "You Took My Sunshine With You" (Decca 5933), and "Got Ramblin' And Gamblin' On My Mind" (Decca 5943), whose romantic verses made them radio-friendly. However, none delivered a hit. Decca presented the York Brothers in the highest audio fidelity available, but the duo dished out less enthusiasm than heard on their Detroit recordings. "Nagging Young Woman," for instance, sounded sedate, compared to the Universal version. However, their restraint suited "I'm Saying Goodbye" (Decca 6018), which exuded a vast sadness that folklorists might trace back centuries to the Old English poem "The Wanderer." Nevertheless, the York Brothers' flawless performances for Decca proved to the world they could stand shoulder-to-shoulder with more famous artists, such as the Shelton Brothers.

After Decca issued their first disc in March, and second in April, the York Brothers hit the Hillbilly Highway, making a triumphant return to Portsmouth, Ohio. Now full-time musicians, they took up residence at the Sylvian restaurant on Scioto Road as a base for nightly performances, and resumed daily broadcasts at WPAY radio.[2]

With the federal government promoting a wartime reduction of civilian travel in order to extend resources such as oil, gasoline, and tires, the York Brothers "played out" the Portsmouth region within several months, and in 1942 they started looking for greener pastures.

---

2. "Mr. Gus J. Johnson Announces that Leslie and George York, heard daily on WPAY at 8:30 A.M., have leased The Sylvian on Scioto Trail." Advertisement for the Sylvian, *Portsmouth Daily Times* (July 18, 1941), 3.

11 | snake bite blues (universal's last yodel)

Until the departure of the York Brothers, they were the only country music act on Universal records. The last known disc pressed with Universal labels, probably manufactured in the early weeks of 1941, seemed an attempt to fulfill demand for more of such music.

How Forest Rye's Red River Blue Yodlers[sp.] came to record "Snake Bite Blues" (Universal 1002), backed with "Don't Come Crying Around Me Mama," is a stumper. However, the group was another "unknown" act; and during those years, they headlined at the Torch Club on East Jefferson and Kitchener, a couple of blocks from Universal Recording Studios, and across from the Hudson Motor Car Company, where Louie Shoun's wife Mabel worked.[1]

Rye grew up in Erin, Tennessee, west of Nashville. Born in 1910, he taught himself to play fiddle, and guitar before leaving home at age fourteen. While Rye was a young boy, champion fiddler Walter Warden, an early influence on "Grand Ole Opry" star Fiddlin' Arthur Smith, lived up the road, in McEwen. Warden thought so highly of Rye, he gave him a fiddle. When Rye came to Detroit in 1924, he spent a week talking his way past a guard into the Ford Motor Company's Highland Park facility, where he learned the artistry of welding.

Rye entertained at house parties through the 1930s, eventually booking evening shows in Detroit cafes and taverns. In 1937 he married, moved back to Erin, and

---

1. "Sons of Detroit Take Pacific Battle Posts," *Detroit Evening Times* (December 11, 1941), 16.

opened a grocery store. He continued visiting friends in Michigan, and in 1939 Rye returned to Detroit, where he resumed the welding trade at Chrysler's facilities on East Jefferson Avenue.

Conrad Brooks, the name of the vocalist on the record label, was a pen name for the churchgoing bandleader. According to Rye's daughter Linda, when he recorded in Detroit during the 1940s, her father used an alias to protect his reputation.[2]

From Rye's first yodel, "Snake Bite Blues," a song about drinking away one's sorrows, sounds like music of 1930, when Jimmie Rodgers was the nation's most popular hillbilly artist. After Rodgers' death in 1933, his unmistakable "blue yodel" persisted through a generation of imitators, including Rye, whose own yodel could strip paint off a wall. Due to the absence of fiddle on the recording, Rye may have strummed the guitar in the style Rodgers himself played, while a steel guitarist turned a standard blues into a Hawaiian swing. The scarcity of copies of this country-Hawaiian crossover, a toned-down cousin to the York Brothers' "Detroit Hulu Girl," probably indicates sales of Rye's first record didn't amount to a hill of beans.

Rye persisted, returning to the Universal studio with more songs in 1942 — a year that proved extraordinary for Shoun and Kiely, and mind-blowing for those of us looking back at the remainders of what appears to have been a year-long party.

---

2. Craig Maki interviewed Linda Rye Austin on June 20, 2012. Interestingly, a Conrad G. Brooks joined the rolls of the AFM Detroit Local 5 union in January 1942 (reported the following month). "Local Reports," *The International Musician* (February 1942. Vol. 40, No. 8), 24.

12 | wayne county blues

In 1941, more than five thousand juke boxes thumped away, in restaurants, taverns, and soda fountains across Wayne, Oakland, and Macomb counties.[1] Record manufacturers distributed one hundred million discs across the United States — impressive, compared to four million just seven years before.[2]

Ed Kiely introduced a new name for his record business: Mellow. Labels of new discs listed Mellow Record Shop, and Mellow Record Company at 965 Dickerson. A year or two later, after Kiely opened a second Mellow Music Shop at 13217 East Jefferson Avenue, selling records, sheet music, instruments, and accessories, he promoted the Dickerson location as "Mellow Music Shop No. 2."

Although Kiely introduced the Mellow Record Company, he dubbed Universal's successor "Hot Wax," with a label design featuring mirrored silhouettes of shapely ladies.[3]

First thing, Kiely reissued "Hamtramck Mama," with "That Nagging Young Husey[sp.]" on its flip side. Red paper labels were printed with gold ink, and included "Manufactured by Mellow Record Shop." Because the York Brothers waxed the tune for Decca, Kiely might have received a cease-and-desist order. He reissued "Hamtramck Mama" backed with "It Tain't No

---

1. Jack Pickering, "City's Juke Boxes Ring the Bell Selling U.S. Defense Bonds," *Detroit Free Press* (September 25, 1941. Vol. 111, No. 144), 1.

2. Selby, op. cit.

3. It appears Hot Wax preceded Mellow labeled discs, as the titles of the last Hot Wax records overlapped with the earliest Mellow labeled records, and all shared the same four-digit master numbers.

Good" — copies of which are more easily found today, than the other.

In the spring of 1941, country music veteran Billy Casteel waxed four tunes at Universal Recording Studios with a group called the Silver Sage Buckaroos. Casteel arrived from East Saint Louis, Illinois, where his group, the Rhythm Cowboys, played in local taverns and broadcast every morning on KXOK radio Venice, Illinois, during 1938-39.[4] Born in 1913 at Wynne, Arkansas, Casteel was known as Therould (Billy) Casteel,[5] and performed in a duo with Roy Meachum, starting in 1925 as the Arkansas Barefoot Boys, then as Zeb and Zeke. After gaining fame on WMC radio Memphis, Tennessee, Zeb and Zeke cut "I'm A Ding Dong Daddy (From Dumas)" and "My Cabin By The Sea" in 1934, issued on Decca 5060.[6] They toured up to Wisconsin, and performed at KXOK before Meachum settled with his family down south in 1939.

Alabama-born Bob Norton led the Silver Sage Buckaroos in Detroit, playing music nightly in local bars. With Norton on bass, the band included a guitarist known as "Slivers," who led a group called the Oregon Buckaroos on WCAR radio Pontiac, Michigan. Another WCAR musician, "Texas" Tony Bigda, played accordion.

---

4. Advertisement for KXOK radio. "One Year of KXOK Performance" *St. Louis Star-Times* (September 19, 1939. Vol. 53, No. 300), 4.

5. In June 1941, "Therould Billy Casteel" was added to the rolls of Detroit musicians union Local No. 5. He was expelled after his army enlistment in 1942, reinstated in 1944, and expelled later the same year. "Local Reports," *The International Musician* (June 1941. Vol. 39, No. 12), 27.

6. On the record, Meachum performed the vocal, fiddle, and whistling.

The group on Casteel's sessions included a remarkable fiddler who played a dirty lowdown blues — possibly Casteel himself, as the fiddle is heard only between vocals. (Or he may have played chop rhythm on a guitar at the session.)

Casteel's first Hot Wax disc (1614) included a re-write of "Hamtramck Mama," titled "Hollywood Mama," with lines such as, "She's a Hollywood Mama / Lordy, how she can love." It's an entertaining romp, but the flip side, "Wayne County Blues," was a bopper *Billboard* described as the "local hit."[7]

In 1940, Michigan Attorney General Thomas Read began investigating bribery, and graft in Wayne County's government.[8] Within a year, former Detroit Mayor Richard W. Reading, Prosecutor Duncan C. McCrea, and dozens of

---

7. They also noted Kiely opened a record shop, where he sold records on his own label to juke box operators. "Amusement Machines (Music)," *Billboard* (July 26, 1941. Vol. 53, No. 30), 78.

8. "Attorney General Installs Aides in McCrea Office to 'Co-Operate'; Groesbeck Offers to Assist Probe," *Detroit Free Press* (February 25, 1940. Vol. 109, No. 297), 1. "Reading Examination Will Commence Today," *Detroit Free Press* (May 4, 1940. Vol. 109, No. 366), 12. "Reading, 22 Others Guilty in Graft Conspiracy Case," *Detroit Free Press* (December 16, 1941. Vol. 110, No. 226), 1.

others were convicted of participating in schemes to ignore illegal activities going on under their noses, in exchange for monthly payoffs. Casteel began "Wayne County Blues" with, "Oh, the judge and the jury, they are nice / They sent us up here for collecting graft on crooked dice / People pay their taxes on their homes / Just to give us money to gamble on / I got the Wayne County blues."

On his second record, Casteel crooned a waltz, "I Wish I Had Never Met You" (Hot Wax 1615), the first slow song Kiely pressed since the York Brothers' "Sweetheart Darling." Its flip side featured another uptempo blues, "Trifling On Me." With a call-and-response refrain, Casteel and band rocked the rhythm as hard as anything the York Brothers had cut previously on East Jefferson.

Casteel's time in Michigan may have included gigs in Port Huron, and Battle Creek, where mentions of a band called the Rhythm Cowboys, the same as Casteel's group back in East Saint Louis, appeared in contemporary newspapers. He enlisted in the Army in 1942. Discharged in 1943, Casteel eventually returned to Arkansas. He died in Missouri in 1972, aged fifty-eight years.

Besides playing a few months in 1947 with the Radio Rangers at KFAB radio Lincoln, Nebraska, Bob Norton continued making music in Detroit watering holes until 1954, when his thirty-four year-old heart unexpectedly quit. A musician whose easygoing outlook, skill, and knowledge of jazz, and western swing won him inspired devotion from contemporaries such as Hal Clark (aka Hal Southern), Eddie Jackson, and Arizona Weston, Norton was buried near Courtland, Alabama, beneath a marker his family etched with an epitaph typical of his dry sense of humor: "Gone, But Not Forgotten."

13 | the hot and mellow year: hot

On December 7, 1941, the Japanese Navy Air Service attacked the United States naval base at Pearl Harbor on the island of Oahu, Hawaii. President Roosevelt asked congress to formally declare war. The day after the attack, two thousand men in Detroit applied to enlist at Army, Navy, and Marine Corps recruitment centers, all of which kept offices open past midnight.[1] Labor unions cancelled planned strikes, and industrial reorganization quickly followed. If factories weren't already retooled for war production, and operating at full capacity, that became a reality within months. Detroit automakers ceased civilian vehicle production by February 9, 1942. Across the nation, demand increased for records to supply juke boxes with music to boost the morale of servicemen, civilians, and war plant employees entering a twenty-four-hour work cycle.

On Monday, May 18, 1942, Detroit newspapers updated readers with the following items: the U.S. government froze prices on most commercial goods, and began rationing tires and gasoline; Chinese soldiers halted Japanese forces in Burma; German troops fought Soviets in Ukraine, and the German Luftwaffe tangled with Britain's Royal Air Force over Occupied France. Out near Ypsilanti, Michigan, Willow Run, the nation's largest industrial plant dedicated to manufacturing weaponry, had recently

---

1. "2,000 in City Apply for Enlistment," *Detroit Free Press* (December 9, 1941. Vol. 111, No. 218), 2.

Forest Rye (top), and Evelyn Haire. *Illustrations by Craig Maki*

started operations.[2] On the same day, but unreported by local news journals, Rye's Red River Blue Yodlers entered Universal Recording Studios to cut two new songs.

"You Had Time To Think It Over," backed with "On Down The Line," were pressed together on Hot Wax (1616). Again, Rye's vocals were credited to Conrad Brooks, and this time he played some fiddle. His band included bass, rhythm guitar, and steel guitar. Rye held back his yodels in favor of a more modern, conversational approach to the tunes. While the A-side's "You Had Time" presented a mournful heart song (and Rye's sad fiddle), "On Down The Line," loosely based on the melody of "It Tain't No Good," included the wily verses loyal customers had come to expect: "She shook it up, she shook it down / She shook it over, and she shook it around / On down the line, on down the line / We got it fixed, on down the line … She took it in the kitchen, and she took it in the hall / She took it on the hill, and took it all …"

If you guessed Rye had a sense of humor, you'd be correct. During the war years, he performed comedy on WSM radio Nashville's "Grand Ole Opry" as Little Willie Rye. All signs point to him as the first Detroit-based entertainer to perform at the "Opry." Rye's reception in Nashville inspired him to relocate to Tennessee in 1944.

In 1947, Rye took a job at the Ford Motor Company's River Rouge Complex in Dearborn, west of Detroit, and built a house in Taylor, Michigan. He soon organized a new band, called the Sage Brush Ranch

---

2. J. Wes Gallagher and Henry Shapiro, "Russians Retake 300 Towns in Assault on Kharkov; Luftwaffe Battles Big RAF Offensive over France," *Detroit Free Press* (May 18, 1942. Vol. 112, No. 14), 1.

Boys, and secured a gig at WXYZ radio Detroit. They worked shows across Southeast Michigan with vocalists Mountain Red (aka Robert Hogg) of Pontiac, and Earl Songer, who also worked at Ford, and recorded for Fortune Records with his guitar-picking wife Joyce. Former Bluebird Records artist Pete Pyle moved next door to Rye, and together they appeared as guests on clear channel WJR radio Detroit's "Big Barn Frolic" Saturday night jamboree. They also cut a split session for Fortune in 1953. Two years later, both the Rye, and Pyle households moved back to Tennessee.

On Nashville radio, and with the band of Big Jeff Bess, Rye resumed his comedy act. He wrote songs, operated a publishing company, and made records. In 1967, Rye took up preaching the lessons of the Bible, which he adopted as his vocation until his death in 1988.

When longtime East Texas resident Evelyn Haire Cicero died in 2018 at age 101, half of her obituary presented tidbits from her life before she married in 1952, including big times in Detroit, and the Midwest.[3] Born in

---

3. Evelyn Jeanette Cicero obituary, https://www.kleinfh.com/obituary/6597967 (Accessed 2021)

1917 in Memphis, Tennessee, Evelyn Haire sang on local radio, starting around 1930. She left Memphis about ten years later, and in April of 1942, performed on WHIP radio Hammond, Indiana, with the Swingtime Cowgirls, a female ensemble she named after Patsy Montana's "Swingtime Cowgirl" record of 1940. Haire's songbook drew heavily from cowboy music played with a swing beat; she even borrowed Montana's 1935 hit "I Want To Be A Cowboy's Sweetheart" as her theme.[4] Probably after their daily gig at WHIP ended (the station closed mid-1942), the Swingtime Cowgirls recorded four sides for Ed Kiely in Detroit.

Although the band — with Haire on bass, Irene Wright on fiddle, Jeanne Lutes on accordion, and a woman named Doris on guitar — lacked the polish of more famous musical acts, Haire's contralto vocals and yodels came across as seasoned and assured. Notably, Haire began three of the four recordings with a variation of, "Howdy folks! This is Evelyn Haire and her Swingtime Cowgirls," as if performing before an audience. Either these were radio trasncriptions, or Haire wanted listeners to know who made the music jumping out of the juke box at the end of the bar.

Their first record (Hot Wax 1617) paired "Prairie Sweetheart," a rambunctious western song with a yodel refrain, and "I Have Done You Wrong," a slow heart song. Although the label read "Hillbilly Novelty," it was the first record Kiely issued where neither side contributed to the pile of salacious songs he'd been selling.

---

4. "Proud of East Texas: GI performer turns 100," KLTV Tyler, Texas (2017) https://www.kltv.com/story/34577003/proud-of-east-texas-gi-performer-turns-100/ (Accessed 2021)

But then ... The Swingtime Cowgirls' next record (Hot Wax 1618) featured "Triflin' Woman," an answer to Billy Casteel's "Trifling On Me," which Haire expressed as a wronged woman out for revenge: "Now my baby trifles on me, I know it's true / What's good for him is good for me, too / I'm triflin' on him," and the ladies in the band shouted, "Triflin' on him!" With a hard-driving rhythm, and Haire growling through the refrains, "Triflin' Woman" bested Casteel's version. "My Pals, My Pinto And I," a breezy, home-on-the-range type song with Haire chirping a bouyant, melodic yodel, appeared on the flip side.

Like the Coon Creek Girls of Renfro Valley, Kentucky, and the Goree All Girl String Band of Huntsville, Texas (a "prison band" of female inmates of the Goree unit at Texas State Penitentiary who performed over WBAP radio Dallas in 1940-44), the Swingtime Cowgirls ranked among the earliest all-female country-western groups. To refine this point, the Coon Creek Girls played traditional music of Appalachia, and Kentucky, making the Swingtime Cowgirls the first western combo of women to appear on commercial records. With these records, Haire and Kiely set a notable precedent, even though each party's goals at the time concerned profits and promotions — cash for Kiely, and an enhanced reputation for Haire as a recording artist.

In a move that failed to help publicize her records in Detroit, the Swingtime Cowgirls turned their wagon back to Chicago, where they made a connection to work tours for the United Service Organizations, traveling the country entertaining American soldiers.

Just before the war ended in 1945, Haire returned to Detroit, where Franny (Westfall) Mitchell, a young woman from West Virginia, replaced the Cowgirls' previous guitarist. "Evelyn was a good entertainer, I'll tell you that. I don't lie about nobody," Mitchell said in 2003.[5] "We worked out at the Wayside, and all over." The Wayside Bowling Bar, north of Detroit in Hazel Park, booked country-western musicians from the 1930s through the 1970s. Demand for entertainers in area clubs remained strong after the war, and Haire spent a couple more years in Detroit.

Mitchell recalled the group started busting its seams when Jeanne Lutes began dating a man of whom Haire, and Wright didn't approve. "There was a musician around — well, he was half-way a musician. His name was Hank Laughlin," said Mitchell. "I always live and let live, and I stood up for Jeanne. They didn't like her, because she took up with that Hank. And he ended up being a stinker, anyway. ... She was from a little town north of Detroit. ... Her family had a great big farm, and they offered to buy her a brand-new car, if she

---

5. Keith Cady interviewed Frances Mitchell (1918-2004) on May 28, 2003.

didn't go with that ol' Hank. He was all pibble-faced, and he didn't know nothing about playing the guitar."

Around 1950, Haire left Detroit fronting a new act, the Evelyn Haire Trio, which included Irene Wright and another woman. For several months, the trio played shows sponsored by agricultural equipment maker International Harvester in rural Ohio, and Indiana. It was during the trio's extended engagement at a Chicago-area venue, when Haire met her future husband. After her marriage, Haire disbanded, and raised a family in California, and Texas, where she died in 2018.[6]

"We played on the radio at that WKMH in Dearborn, one time," said Mitchell. Then she added, with surprise, "And I didn't know they made a record!"

In 1942, after A.R. "Jack" Morey assumed the head of appliances division for Detroit wholesaler Buhl Sons Company, he signed a distribution deal with the Mellow Record Company. With Michigan offices in Detroit and Grand Rapids, and another in Toledo, Ohio, Buhl Sons covered a large territory, sending hardware, textiles, seed, carpets, radios, and other household goods to stores across the Midwest. Buhl Sons had been a longtime phonograph machine distributor, and Morey used this network to sell records, as wartime shortages caused other items to become difficult — impossible, in many cases — to obtain.

While strong demand for records continued, the United States government diverted all virgin shellac, a

---

6. Coincidentally, Haire lived in Tomball, Texas, near the Huntsville prison that once housed the Goree Girls.

main ingredient for making records, into war production. Most shellac was sourced from Southeast Asia, an area then controlled by the Empire of Japan. By the end of the year, the U.S. government officially eliminated private access to shellac, for the duration. Some record makers experimented with using other types of plastics, but most resorted to recycling old discs to press new music. Pressing plants eventually required record companies to send them quotas of old records to recycle with their orders.

Around the time when Kiely signed the deal with Buhl Sons, singer Kate Smith, a famous entertainer of stage, records, and radio, with support from her show business friends, sponsored a public entreaty that appeared in newspapers across the country, soliciting donations to meet a goal of collecting thirty-seven million unwanted phonograph records.[7] The idea was to sell old discs to record manufacturers for pennies, to purchase record players, and make new records for American troops serving overseas. By the following year, juke box companies, appliance shops, and enterprises such as Grinnell Brothers music stores, and the J.L. Hudson department store in downtown Detroit, got into the act, offering a nickel per pound to customers who delivered "scrap records," for the purpose of recycling the materials into new discs.

These drives attracted considerable participation from the public, which made the number of records Kiely pressed in 1942 — we're not done counting, yet! — even more surprising.

---

7. Kate Smith, "Your Old Records Will Buy New Ones for Fighting Men," *Detroit Free Press* (June 28, 1942. Vol. 112, No. 55), 37.

The York Brothers, with Johnnie Lavender at center, circa 1943. *Image source: Craig Maki, courtesy John Bell*

14 | the hot and mellow year: mellow

With a second edition of Forest Rye's Hot Wax record (the band's name on the label changed to Rye's Blue Yodlers) and through *seventeen* more releases, the Buhl Sons Company name and office locations graced the labels of most of Kiely's records.

After the Swingtime Cowgirls discs appeared on Hot Wax, Kiely started making records with the more wholesome "Mellow" brand. The premier Mellow labeled records included a third pressing of Rye's "On Down The Line," and second pressings of Evelyn Haire's records. After those releases, the new label — with its hand-drawn, art deco font displaying "MELLOW" above the record hole, and a drawing of a bluebird perched atop a leafy branch, its beak spouting a stream of musical notes drifting down over its tail feathers — represented only "Hillbilly Novelty" or "Hillbilly Blues" records "By YORK BROS."

Because of materials shortages, major labels, including Decca, dropped many acts in 1942, and the York Brothers joined this company. After Decca issued a third disc from the 1941 session (Decca 6018 "My Little Honeysuckle Rose" backed with "I'm Saying Goodbye") in early 1942, George York and family left Portsmouth for Detroit. Brother Les stayed put, performing with other musicians at the Sylvian, and WPAY radio. His musical pals included a young barber named Virgil Frazie, who picked guitar, and sang lead and harmony; and Johnnie Lavender, a bassist from nearby Ironton, Ohio. Due to an episode of rickets during infancy, Lavender's spine had grown arched. His stage performances included comedy, dressed as a cartoonish, backwoods rube — a role often played by hillbilly bass players of the era. Before Les returned to Detroit that summer, he may have invited Frazie, and Lavender to follow him north. Frazie, however, enlisted in the Navy. Married, and classified IV-F by the military, Lavender organized and conducted his own band in Portsmouth.

Les York arrived in Detroit with a grip of new songs, and an electronic pickup mounted across the sound hole of his guitar. When the York Brothers revisited Universal Recording Studios, they carried themselves with the practiced confidence of professionals, and delivered the kinds of songs that Decca Records would have approved — no more double-entendres or risqué lyrics. If Kiely had reservations about a move away from bawdy novelties, the York Brothers proved him wrong.

Their reappearance on East Jefferson Avenue heralded a creative run that included thirty-six more (documented) recordings. From the York Brothers' earliest discs, Les experimented with a variety of ideas, with few songs sounding alike. Now he expanded his subjects and styles. Mellow 1619 through 1625 featured the two brothers playing an "electrified folk music," with Les playing lead guitar through a small speaker (or amplifier), and George strumming rhythm on his acoustic guitar. Despite the resulting separation of guitar sonance, the brothers' vocals blended together more beautifully than ever, as they rendered tender love songs ("Blue Skies Turned To Gray," "I'll Be Happy Again," "Just Wanting You"), and uptempo blues ("I Don't Want No Part Of You," "Long Gone," "Life Can Never Be The Same") with zeal. They also waxed cowboy songs ("Riding And Singing My Song" and "Going Back To The Sunny South"), revisited patriotic themes ("Hail, Hail Ol' Glory" and "Hillbilly Rose"), and even delivered a chant of excited anticipation to return to a faraway home ("We're Gonna Catch That Train"), a pleasant fantasy for folks stuck in place because of wartime travel restrictions.

In September, *Billboard* magazine mentioned Ed Kiely had registered as sole owner of the Mellow Record Company.[1] Around that time, Johnnie Lavender joined the York Brothers in Detroit. He contributed a percussive, "slap" technique on string bass that changed the trio's subsequent Mellow records into a new dance music that couldn't be defined strictly as old-time, western swing, or proto-bluegrass. With a style often heard in recordings by small swing and blues combos, Lavender's performances introduced a solid, rocking rhythm that propelled the York Brothers' music into previously unmapped territory, and also characterized the act's sound for years to come. Combining Lavender's bass with George's rhythm picking, and the electrified guitar runs worked up by Les, the trio developed a singular, stripped-down sound in Detroit — a dozen years before Elvis Presley, and Johnny Cash used the same "two guitars and bass" instrumentation on their early recordings at Sun Records in Memphis, Tennessee.

Music writers of the mid-1950s employed the term "rockabilly" to describe country musicians playing the new

---

1. "Market Reports—August Biz Good," *Billboard* (September 12, 1942. Vol. 54, No. 36), 75.

rock'n'roll style. But during the heyday of Detroit's Arsenal of Democracy, with jumping numbers such as "Going To The Shindig," "I Got My Eyes On You," and a faster remake of "Hamtramck Mama," the York Brothers indeed played rockabilly in wartime Detroit. Add a tape loop echo (a common feature of 1950s rock records) to the tracks I just mentioned, and you'll hear what I mean.

Frustrated by juke box operators and radio stations that didn't pay royalties to the American Federation of Musicians, its president James Petrillo ordered a recording ban that lasted from August 1942 until the end of 1943. The York Brothers, or Kiely, may have been making too much money to pay it attention. Kiely kept the trio busy with more sessions that produced "New Trail To Mexico," and "Rose Of The Rio Grande," both of which could have been featured in singing cowboy movies. "York Brothers Blues," and "Got To Get Rid Of My Worried Mind" expressed the melancholy and frustrations of living, and loving. "Mother's Sunny Smile," and "Kentucky's Calling Me" proclaimed devotion to past memories of family. And "A Merry Christmas To The Boys Over There" signaled support by the home front to the American men fighting with Allied forces across the globe.

In December, *Billboard* noted, "The Detroit area is paying plenty of nickels to hear the York Brothers' *Not Over 35*."[2] Starting with the wail of a police car siren, this talking blues (Mellow 1641-B), on the flip side of "A Merry Christmas To The Boys Over There" (Mellow 1640-A)

---

2. "American Folk Records," *Billboard* (December 26, 1942. Vol. 54, No. 52), 64.

made light of the thirty-five miles-per-hour wartime limit on private vehicle speeds to conserve gas and tires, while celebrating the equal treatment under the law of "big shots" in limousines and more humble folk.

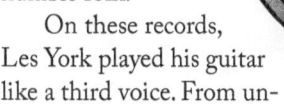

On these records, Les York played his guitar like a third voice. From uncluttered melodies, to syncopated solos crackling through his small amplifier, he expertly played around the meter with twangy declarations of hot desire, desolate longing, dazzling optimism — often jammed together in the same song — that listeners heard, and felt. No other country guitarist in Detroit could touch his boots.

As business boomed across America (the S&P 500 stock market index grew by fifteen percent in 1942), Kiely issued what wax hounds considered the Mellow Record Company's swan song: the rocking "I Got My Eyes On You" backed with "You'll Pay For It All" (Mellow 1642). For decades, devotees of all things Mellow (all both of us) believed Kiely, Shoun, and the York Brothers ended their collaborations on that high note. Seventy years later though, I got hold of a short stack of discs with worn, plain white labels, and I raised a glass of Michigan-made lager, toasting "Opportunity" for proving this idea false.

Label of Mellow 1666-A "You Lied To Me," published by Dixie Music as "You're Going Away" in 1944

The flip (blank) side of a disc also had a white paper label stamped "Mellow Record Co. / 965 Dickerson Ave., / Phone Murray 747 Detroit, Mich."

15 | mellow songs to remember

From 1943 to 1947, one could easily find printed transcriptions of York Brothers songs in books, as well as in music inserts of the *Mountain Broadcast and Prairie Recorder*, a short-lived magazine that documented country and western music performers across North America. In 1943, and again after the war ended, Dixie Music Publishing Company of New York City printed editions of a "York Brothers Famous Folio of Songs to Remember," which featured their Mellow recordings.[1] The front cover of the first edition presented the York Brothers in dark silk cowboy shirts and white hats, along with Johnnie Lavender, seated between them, wearing a polka-dotted shirt, a worn hat, and holding his string bass (*see page 74*).

York Brothers songs also appeared in "Buddy Starcher's Famous Folio of Songs to Remember" of 1943.[2] Dixie Music often filled out their books with numbers that weren't written by the cover artists, which happened in both the Starcher, and York Brothers folios. The publisher also peppered York Brothers compositions through a series of volumes titled "Songs of the Mountains and Prairies."

Dixie Music printed (at least) thirty-four songs by the York Brothers in several books — including five songs that haven't turned up on records. In fact, it would

---

1. *York Brothers Famous Folio of Songs to Remember*, (New York: Dixie Music Publishing Company, 1943 (first edition), and 1946)

2. Buddy Starcher (1906-2001) gained fame for his song "I'll Still Write Your Name In The Sand" in 1949, and earned a hit with "History Repeats Itself" in 1966.

be seven, instead of five, if a grimy heap of one-sided 78s hadn't arrived at my doorstep ten years ago.

In recent York Brothers and Mellow discographies, five records in my bundle were undocumented. Someone (Shoun? Kiely?) had written details of each disc in pencil on white paper labels that, these many years later, displayed scars of water and mildew damage across their faces. Because most juke boxes before 1950 played only one side of records, these one-sided discs may have served as promotional pressings, or reference copies.[3] The last commercial Mellow record by the York Brothers was numbered 1642 (-A and -B). The mystery discs began with 1662-A and ended with 1666-A (with numbers missing from the sequence). While none of these recordings were pressed on two-sided commercial records, I found three of them transcribed in books published by Dixie Music (*see sections III, IV, and V in Discographies*).

In September 1943, *Billboard* printed a letter in the "American Folk Tunes and Tunesters" column, signed by A Good Old Hillbilly from Kentucky.[4] The writer explained, "I came to Detroit in 1942 and am now in a war plant. When night time comes and I get off from work I go to a place called Jefferson Inn where I find real old-time music as put on by the York Brothers. ... The boys have made 135 records and are fine in their playing of old-time music. They are now broadcasting over WJLB, Detroit, four times a week." One hundred thirty-five records must

---

3. They are definitely not lacquer coated discs.
4. "American Folk Tunes and Tunesters," *Billboard* (September 11, 1943. Vol. 55, No. 37), 63.

have been a typo. Thirty-five aligns more with current York Brothers discographies (*see Discographies*).

While Petrillo's recording ban was in effect, major labels kept record factories churning out new platters with raw or recycled materials, issuing music that artists had cut before the ban. According to law, by December 1942 Ed Kiely's record manufacturer could no longer access virgin shellac. Around this time, Kiely stopped ordering new records in quantity. Evidence for this is heard in the next-to-last commercial Mellow disc, "A Merry Christmas To The Boys Over There," in which the York Brothers expressed hope for the war to end in 1943. After (or during) the recording ban, Kiely and/or the York Brothers might have paid for sessions that resulted in small orders of one-sided discs, such as the records described above. In 1944, Dixie Music published three titles found among my stack.

As the war overseas intensified, the fortunes of the York Brothers improved. In May 1943, they began an exclusive engagement at the aforementioned Jefferson Inn, at 11707 East Jefferson Avenue, near the Chrysler factory. Owner William Levin opened the club in October 1941 with vaudeville entertainment. By 1943 Levin realized the surrounding neighborhood, as well as his patrons, consisted mostly of workers from the South. The York Brothers shared a stage with the Jefferson Inn's house orchestra, and a rotating cast of entertainers, such as musical chefs, a dog circus, acrobats, and trick bull trainer Tex Moseley with "Ferdinand the Bull" from Hollywood, California. They also broadcast on WJLB radio Detroit, sponsored by Koppitz Beer.[5] By the time the York Brothers enlisted in the U.S. Navy — George in January 1944, and Les two months later — each was making $115 a week at the Jefferson Inn, during a time when enlisted servicemen received thirty to fifty dollars per month. The Navy sent George to the Pacific Theater, and Les to the Atlantic.

Having led his own band before joining the York Brothers in Detroit, Johnnie Lavender continued entertaining at the Jefferson Inn, fronting the Rocky Mountain Ramblers.[6] His group included left-handed guitarist Doyle Starnes, William H. Taft "Rosebud" Blevins on steel, and Franny Mitchell on rhythm guitar.[7]

Around Christmas, Lavender took a break from the Jefferson Inn to visit family back home in Ironton, Ohio. He may have been ill when he left Detroit, because in January 1945, Lavender died from a severe case of pneumonia at his parents' house. He was thirty years old.

---

5. During its early years, WJLB brokered time on its airwaves, presenting a variety of musical programming, and local interest talk shows.

6. "American Folk Tunes and Tunesters," *Billboard* (February 12, 1944. Vol. 56, No. 7), 67.

7. Doyle Starnes (1910-1976), a fixture in Detroit taverns featuring country music, from the 1930s until his death, hailed from Baxter, Tennessee. Taft Blevins (1910-1957), a popular steel guitarist in local bars, and radio, died in a suspicious accident at his home in Detroit. Hearsay blamed it on a man with whom his wife was friendly. For more about Franny Mitchell, see: Craig Maki and Keith Cady, *Detroit Country Music: Mountaineers, Cowboys, and Rockabillies* (Ann Arbor: University of Michigan Press, 2013).

16 | mellow times

After Allied victories over the Axis in 1945, *Billboard* mentioned Kiely a few more times.

January 1946 — "... Edward Kiely is also in the record manufacturing business under the firm name Mellow Music Company. He plans to have his labels in quantity pressing soon."[1] George York received his Navy discharge in November 1945, and Les in January 1946. They regrouped in Detroit, playing gigs with Warren Henry "Swanny" Swann on bass, before the trio moved to Nashville, later that year. Detroit musician Hubert (Hugh) Friar said the York Brothers recorded for the Mellow Record Company "after they got out of the Navy."[2] The whereabouts of such recordings, if they exist, are a mystery.

August 1946 — "Edward Kiely, juke box operator, is readying his own line of records for the market. They will be labeled Mellow Records."[3] Despite the manufacturing sector's swivel to producing civilian goods, Kiely seemed to have trouble restarting his label. He issued one commercial record after the war ended, though. Labels of Mellow 1638, "Going To The Shindig," backed with "Mother's Sunny Smile," appeared with notable differences from the labels of Mellow records numbered before and after it. A typeset address of the Mellow Music Shop (13217 East Jefferson Avenue) appeared at top, with no

---

1. "Retail Platters," *Billboard* (January 19, 1946. Vol. 58, No. 3), 81.

2. Hubert Friar (1927-2020) interviewed by Keith Cady on January 24, 2001.

3. "Coinmen You Know," *Billboard* (August 31, 1946. Vol. 58, No. 35), 120.

mention of 965 Dickerson, suggesting the record was made after Kiely's interest in that location ended in 1947 (*see below*); the labels credited "York Brothers" instead of "York Bros."; the Buhl Sons Company attribution disappeared;[4] and the labels were printed with gold ink on red paper, instead of silver ink on black paper, like all other Mellow records. Also of note, Kiely issued recordings made before the York Brothers enlisted in the Navy. Not only do the catalog numbers indicate this, during the introduction of "Going To The Shindig," Les York calls out to Johnnie Lavender, who responds with a joyful cackle.

March 1947 — "Edward Kiely of the Mellow Music Company was recently stabbed and robbed of $185 by a pair of bandits."[5] The juke box business was not all beer and skittles.

June 1950 — "Edward Kiely, pioneer music operator ... reports business slowly coming out of a three-month standstill caused by the long Chrysler strike."[6]

In 1947, after changing its name to Globe Music Company, Kiely sold his shop at 965 Dickerson to Arthur Genzburg, a longtime seller of radio, records, and music appliances in the city.[7] Shoun continued operating his radio

---

4. Buhl Sons Company, which in 1947 signed a deal with Columbia Records, continued distributing records across the Midwest after the war. However, *Billboard* didn't list Mellow among its affiliated labels.

5. "Coinmen You Know," *Billboard* (March 22, 1947. Vol. 59, No. 12), 111.

6. "Coinmen You Know," *Billboard* (June 24, 1950. Vol. 62, No. 25), 171.

7. *Musical Merchandise Combined for the Duration [with] The Music Trade Review*. News coverage from Oct. 1946 to Sept. 1947 (1946-47. Vols. 43-44), 32.

and TV repair business at the same address. In September 1949, Kiely's and Shoun's names appeared together on a passenger list for a flight from Mexico City to Houston, Texas. I could find no clue as to the purpose of the trip.[8]

The York Brothers signed with Bullet Records of Nashville, Tennessee, in 1946. After waxing twelve sides for Bullet, the Yorks joined King Records of Cincinnati, Ohio, in 1947. At their first King session, they cut tunes originally issued by Mellow. Except for "It Tain't No Good," none were released — probably because Dixie Music held publishing rights for most of the Detroit records, and Syd Nathan, head of King Records, preferred to issue music with his own publishing and copyrights.

When stage managers discovered Les York with a bottle of spirits backstage at the "Grand Ole Opry," WSM sent him packing. George followed his brother to KWKH radio's "Louisiana Hayride," in Shreveport, Louisiana, before they shifted gears back to the Motor City in 1949, where they played music at night, and bet on horse races during the day. That year, Fortune Records reissued "Conscription Blues," retitled "Calling Me,"[9] on

---

8. Ancestry.com, *Texas, U.S., Arriving and Departing Passenger and Crew Lists, 1893-1963* [database online]. Provo, UT, USA: Ancestry.com Operations, Inc., 2014. (Accessed 2021)

9. The A-side of Rialto 118, "You Are My Sunshine" by Cliff and His Cowboys, was a remake of Governor Jimmie Davis' 1940 hit song. A copy I reviewed was autographed by "Cliff J. Braun" — probably Clifford J. Braun (1908-1962) who ran the Automatic Sales Company (juke boxes and vending machines) of 1300 Sylvania Ave., Toledo, Ohio. The autograph matched Braun's signature on his 1940 draft registration card. This record was a custom pressing by Jack Brown; its number fit neatly within the Fortune catalog.

a subsidiary label dubbed Rialto (118), and the Universal masters of "Hamtramck Mama" and "Highland Park Girl" together on one Fortune disc (120).

After launching Fortune with big band recordings in 1946, Jack and Devora Brown started adding country music a couple of years later. Jack Brown probably received the early York Brothers Universal masters from Shoun around 1949. Brown registered the publishing rights to the songs that he reissued, and because it continued to sell, he kept the 1939 version of "Hamtramck Mama" in print through the 1960s.

A scenario of Brown buying a handful of Universal masters from Shoun could point to the origin of the Shoun Brothers mystery. Perhaps Shoun made a copy of the Shelton Brothers record, creating a new master for practice with his equipment, or to bootleg the disc for the juke box trade. "Shelton Bros" in cursive scrawl, the most common handwriting style of the era, could be misread as "Shoun Bros," especially if smudged. Or maybe the only name written on the master was "Shoun." Brown probably wasn't aware of the Shelton Brothers, and if he knew Shoun well, he might have been inclined to interpret the credit as "Shoun Brothers."

When he passed Universal masters to Brown, a couple of which Kiely had reissued on Mellow, Shoun may have caused a rift with his former colleague. Kiely kept a tight grip on Mellow masters and none were reissued in his lifetime. In fact, Brown waited until after Kiely's death to release more recordings the York Brothers made at Universal.

In 1953, King Records released "Tennessee Tango" by the York Brothers, and it climbed country-western music sales charts across America. Later that year, the York Brothers moved to Dallas, Texas, where George opened his own tavern. They spent time in Detroit during the summer of 1954, appearing on WJR radio's "Goodwill Jamboree" Saturday nights with Casey Clark's Lazy Ranch Boys, as well as other venues during the week. Brown reissued "Detroit Hulu Girl" backed with "Going Home" (Fortune 180) that year. After their move, and through the 1960s, the York Brothers often appeared on radio in the Dallas/Fort Worth region, as well as on television shows, including Red Foley's widely syndicated "Ozark Jubilee" during the 1950s.

Few other recordings captured the vitality the York Brothers expressed in their Detroit-made discs.[10] Still, they created a substantial legacy of music after Mellow: for Bullet (twelve sides), King (sixty-six!), Decca (one more single in 1957), Sage ("I'll Cry Again Tomorrow," a solo effort by Les, sold well, and was even covered by Bob Wills' band for Liberty Records), and their own York Records during the 1960s; until George grew ill, and died in 1974.

---

10. In 2001, Tommy Venable (1927-2008), another York Brothers bassist, told Keith Cady that, with few exceptions, after the first session for King Records, Les wasn't allowed to play lead guitar in the studio when they recorded for the label. He played lead on sessions for other labels, such as Sage, and his own York Records. The York Brothers came closest to capturing the exuberance of their Detroit records on a "live" album called "Country Comedy" (Karavan 102) they made during the 1960s.

Every summer from 1956 through the 1960s (with a lengthier stay in 1957) Les peformed in Detroit without George, hitting local stages, and radio (WBRB Mount Clemens) with local singer Danny Richards and his band. A brave talent, whose unique songwriting, singing, and guitar picking articulated the lives, emotions, and humor of a vanished generation of Detroiters, Les York passed away in Texas, ten years after George.

From the mid-1940s, before audio tape was widely available, this eight-inch lacquer coated disc (some were also made in the standard ten-inch dimension), manufactured as a Capitol Records promotion, was sold by the Mellow Music Shop for making home recordings.

Charlie Jones and his Kentucky Corn Crackers at WEXL radio Royal Oak, Michigan, about 1936. Wearing a black hat, Jones holds a fiddle, second from left. William Guy Oatsvall leans against the wall at right. Behind the microphone at far left is WEXL Program Director Kirk Knight. The two musicians at center are unknown. *Image source: Craig Maki, courtesy Gary Oatsvall*

17 | beyond mellow

Although Kiely took over the record business associated with Universal Recording Studios, Shoun may have continued making custom recordings for new clients who walked through his doors. Let's tear through some possibilities. (*Also see section VII of Discographies.*)

In January 1942, retired major league baseball umpire George Moriarty, and pianist, singer, and orchestra leader Carl Bonner, introduced a baseball-themed war tune to news reporters in Detroit.[1] "You're Gonna Win That Ball Game Uncle Sam" attracted mentions in sports pages around the country. The Four Dukes, a vocal quartette, waxed it for a Detroit label called Peaka. (The flip side, a Moriarty composition titled "Mammy's Little Blackout Baby" didn't age well, from birth.) Shoun might have recorded the Four Dukes, as the master numbers followed his four-digit format (6500 and 6501), and the Peaka labels included the same reference to Buhl Sons Company, as Mellow records.

West Kentucky native Charlie Jones and his Kentucky Corn Crackers cut a series of traditional fiddle tunes, heart songs, and popular melodies with western styled arrangements in 1947-48. Again, the master numbers were four digits, spanning 1782 to 1789 (A and B sides for each number, sixteen in total).

---

1. "Baseball Provides Theme for New War Song," *Detroit Free Press* (January 25, 1942. Vol. 111, No. 266), 10.

Born in 1893, Jones grew up with eight siblings on his family's farm near Dunmor, Kentucky, in Muhlenberg County. He took up the fiddle, and worked in a coal mine until World War I, when he moved to Detroit. A factory laborer by day, Jones and his group began performing music at night on WMBC radio Detroit, in 1926. During the late 1920s, Chief Redbird sat in, playing fiddle, banjo, and guitar. A member of Otto Gray's Oklahoma Cowboys show band, which originated in Stillwater, Oklahoma, Redbird was probably passing time between gigs.[2]

Jones married his second wife in 1929, and in 1930 he moved his group to WJBK radio Detroit, with sponsorship by Bill Reading's Reading Credit Clothing Company on Washington Boulevard, downtown. William Guy Oatsvall, who had performed on an all-request music program as a "mystery voice" at WJR, joined the Kentucky Corn Crackers to sing, play banjo, and guitar.[3] In 1936, Jones, who'd married his third wife, moved the group north of Detroit to WEXL radio Royal Oak, retaining Bill Reading's sponsorship. After more than a dozen years in radio, in 1939, Jones and the Kentucky Corn Crackers signed off, and devoted themselves individually to the war effort.

Jones pulled together new ensembles after the war, and in 1947 they made two records for the short-lived Arcadia label, one of several new record companies in

---

2. Chief Redbird's scrapbooks included newspaper clippings announcing his guest appearances with the Kentucky Corn Crackers at WMBC radio. As they toured during the 1920s, the Oklahoma Cowboys performed over WJR, and WWJ radio in Detroit.

3. Gary Oatsvall interviewed by Craig Maki in March 2019, and August 2021, by email.

Detroit. Each disc paired a vocal by Bill Hicks with an instrumental led by Jones and his fiddle.[4] Another new label, Vargo Records of Owosso, Michigan, reissued these, and pressed the rest of the Kentucky Corn Crackers recordings with its brand at its Owosso factory.

The next two platters — arguably the best instrumentals by the group — presented high-energy performances that included whoops and shouting. "Gray Eagle" backed with "Pulling The Bow" (Vargo 29033) sounded like such a party, Jones might have invited his old pal Chief Redbird to the session.

The final four Vargo records by Jones and company featured more modern sounds, including the George Sikes Trio, led by Missouri-born George Washington Sikes, along with his sons Olace ("Bud"), and George Jr. ("Lucky").[5] The Sikes men worked at Ford Motor Company, and participated in Ford musical units, besides broadcasting the "Uncle George" show at WEXL, during the war. (Lucky Sikes eventually led his own band

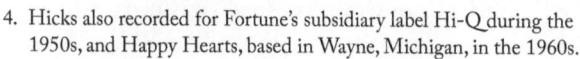

---

4. Hicks also recorded for Fortune's subsidiary label Hi-Q during the 1950s, and Happy Hearts, based in Wayne, Michigan, in the 1960s.

5. Craig Maki communicated with Lea Ann Nall-Williams via electronic message in August 2020, and October 2021.

in Flint, Michigan.) One Kentucky Corn Crackers disc presented two traditional instrumentals, and the other three paired an instrumental with a vocal side by the trio. For example, on one disc, the trio crooned a remake of the hit "New San Antonio Rose" backed with a polka led by accordionist Micky Wionesk. Two other instrumentals spotlighted guitarist Bob Turner picking pop standards, such as "Sweet Georgia Brown." The Rondo label, based in Chicago, Illinois, reissued twelve Vargo sides by the Kentucky Corn Crackers in 1949-51, after Vargo ceased production, and Rondo acquired the masters.

I asked Oatsvall's son about the studio where the Kentucky Corn Crackers recorded. Unable to recall a name, he said, "it would have been on the east side of town." One of the earliest country and folk artists of Detroit radio and records, Charlie Jones died in September 1967, aged seventy-four, in Trenton, Michigan, and was buried at Glenwood Cemetery, in Wayne.

Elton Adams, another fiddle player from West Kentucky, appeared on local records at the same time as the Kentucky Corn Crackers. In 1947, he and his Blue Ridge Mountaineers released four sides with master numbers 1802 through 1806 (1805 is presumed lost). Adams made two instrumentals, and two vocals with a man named Red Nix, including "Good Old Mountain Dew," for Arcadia, later reissued on Vargo. (As with Vargo sides by the Kentucky Corn Crackers, Rondo reissued a couple of Adams' sides.) The guitarist with the Blue Ridge Mountaineers sounded like "Butterfingers" Bob Turner, featured on the last records by the Kentucky Corn Crackers.

Born in Crofton, Kentucky, in 1903, Adams lived in Dearborn, Michigan, by the mid-1930s. Like Forest Rye, he worked as a welder at the Ford River Rouge Complex. Standing six feet tall, with black hair and blue eyes, Adams and his fiddle often enlivened Ford employee picnics, where he met Fortune Records artists Earl and Joyce Songer. Adams' last known recordings included a no-holds-barred performance of the traditional "Fox Chase," at a 1950 recording session with the Songers.[6] During the 1960s, Adams and his wife returned to Kentucky, where he died in 1971.

Even if Shoun and Kiely did not play a role in making these records, their endeavors established an independent record company could succeed in Detroit. And it was accomplished with decidedly non-mainstream music — particularly country music, which began a grand expansion in popular American culture during the 1930s via cowboy movies, and radio. From the early 1940s through the 1950s, pop stars often recorded big

---

6. "Fox Chase" backed with "Will There Be Any Flowers On Your Grave?" appeared on Fortune 131 by Earl Songer and his Rocky Road Ramblers.

band arrangements of hit country songs, until country itself started crossing over into the pop sales category, by the end of the 1950s.

Was there an audio "style" associated with Universal Recording Studios? Perhaps. The country musicians performed as they would during public shows, by including asides, and hollering during their "hillbilly blues" recording sessions. Unlike established acts on records, they played music as they felt it, without much, if any, direction from anyone who wasn't directly participating. At Universal, the York Brothers shed the formality they affected for other record companies, and performed the emotions suggested by their song narratives as if living them in the moment. Years after the war, independent labels such as Sun Records in Memphis, Tennessee; Chess in Chicago, Illinois; and Fortune in Detroit teased out similar performances from their artists (mostly blues, vocal groups, rock'n'roll, and country artists). For several years during the 1950s, records made at these small studios chased the major labels, racing up country, rhythm and blues, and even pop music sales charts.

During the era when juke boxes held their greatest influence on the music business, Harry Graham, Louie Shoun, and Ed Kiely showed a way for post-war businessmen who studied their playbook. For instance, Jack Brown of Fortune Records sold discs to juke box operators. And after releasing a few pop recordings, Brown turned to country numbers with bawdy titles, such as "The Tattooed Lady," and "The Dirty Boogie." Brown even re-issued the original "Hamtramck Mama." Shoun and Kiely must have noticed Brown's success, but they didn't have much time left to ponder their place in history.

18 | east side boosters

Recidivism rates of Michigan parolees during the first half of the 20th century averaged forty to fifty percent.[1] Once freed from Leavenworth prison, Kiely avoided adding to those statistics. No doubt it wasn't easy, because the juke box business seemed rife with corruption.

As far back as the 1920s, John Marquette had run-ins with Detroit police over mechanical games, and whether he had placed them lawfully in beer gardens. During the 1930s, punks posing as collectors for juke box operators often stole coins from machines. During the 1940s, the federal government began monitoring and investigating criminal activities involving mafia, and gang infiltrations of vending machine labor unions. So-called "union representatives," and sometimes corrupt police officers, harassed unaffiliated juke box operators as well as tavern owners, stealing from machines, replacing non-union machines without notice, picketing bar entrances — even bombing places of business when words (or threats) failed to persuade proprietors to "join the racket."

When Harry Graham transferred his Wurlitzer accounts to Detroit's Italian mafia during the war, it was a sign of things to come. Through the next dozen years, mafia influence over Detroit's vending machine businesses grew so pervasive, it attracted numerous federal investigations.

Kiely seemed to have kept bad elements of the business at arm's length. I couldn't find evidence he was ever

---

1. "Half State Convicts Were 'In' Before," *Livingston County Daily Press and Argus* (October 2, 1940. Vol. 94, No. 11), 6.

Ten-inch wide record bags from the Mellow Music Shop, early 1950s

called to testify, or even mentioned, during government hearings into organized crime and the juke box industry.

In 1948, Jimmy Work, an amiable musician from Dukedom, Kentucky, who moved to Detroit during the war, visited Kiely at the Mellow Music Shop on East Jefferson. Work made the rounds of Detroit juke box operators to sell copies of his new record, "Tennessee Border," the original version of what became a hit song for a herd of country artists, such as Red Foley, and Tennessee Ernie Ford, when they covered it the following year. Ben Okum, another Detroit vending machine operator, co-produced the recording for his new Alben label. Kiely bought a box of Work's 78s. "He was an older fella," Work recalled in 2012, "and a real nice guy."[2]

Work added that Kiely sold Mellow records to Walter Drake, who ran Drake's Record Shop up Jefferson Avenue at St. Jean.[3] For several years, Drake supported local country musicians by selling their platters to juke box record distributors in Ohio, Kentucky, West Virginia, and other southern states. (No doubt Drake's sales helped "Tennessee Border" attract the attention of Decca Records, who signed Work to a contract in 1949.)

By the start of the 1950s, Kiely held leadership positions, such as director, and vice president, in the east side chapter of the Detroit Lions Club. In January 1951,

---

2. Craig Maki interviewed Jimmy Work (1924-2018) on July 25, 2012.
3. Drake opened his business after the war ended, and promoted and sponsored country music shows in Detroit. In 1954, he sold out. In March 1955, a mysterious fire wrecked the shop.

business owners in Kiely's neighborhood elected him president of the East Jefferson Boosters, a committee that promoted local merchants.[4] This act seemed like a public acknowledgment that, at age fifty-five, Kiely had turned his life around.

In 1953, a month after his fifty-seventh birthday, a heart attack struck down the chief booster. Kiely's fourth wife, twenty-three year-old Lula Jane, buried him at White Chapel Memorial Park in Troy, Michigan, along Crooks Road. She remarried and, in May 1954, sold the Mellow Record Shop to Louis Chiodo.[5] He kept the store's name, and conferred management to his son Ross.[6] While pushing pop records, the Chiodos slowly sold off Mellow stock — documents of Detroit's wartime folkways encoded in grooves of once-precious shellac, purchased by resident York Brothers fans who remembered the music that illuminated a dark time with empathy, and hope.

After a lengthy illness, former "Mr. Music" Harry G. Graham died in December 1954, aged sixty-nine.

In January 1955, the *Detroit Free Press*, *Detroit News*, and *Detroit Times* reported Louie Shoun's death from lung

---

4. "Chief Booster," *Detroit Free Press* (January 18, 1951. Vol. 120, No. 258), 17.

5. Joe Martin, "Dealer Doings," *Billboard* (May 22, 1954. Vol. 66, No. 21), 61.

6. In 1957 Ross Chiodo studied theatre at Wayne State University. He moved to New York City and, using the name Ross Gifford, appeared in productions such as "Fiddler On The Roof." In 1977, as he was strolling through Manhattan, an assailant with a knife took his life. "Obituaries," *Detroit Free Press* (Nov. 8, 1977. Vol. 147, No. 188), 6-B.

cancer, at age sixty-one. Although the papers cited his radio and television repair business on Dickerson Avenue, none mentioned the pioneering punch of Universal Recording Studios.[7] Following a memorial service at the DeSantis Funeral Home at Charlevoix and Chalmers streets, Shoun's family buried him at Roseland Park Cemetery, along Woodward Avenue in Berkley, Michigan.

All Star TV, based on East Warren, purchased Shoun's enterprise at 965 Dickerson, and re-opened it as a second location, offering small appliance repair services, while Globe Music continued selling records, before a deluge of decades erased the shopping district of these stories. Now, towering over modern, far-flung structures — a drug store franchise, a bank, a strip mall, a high school technical career center — stands the nine-story brick shell of the Hotel Savarine, built a century ago as a residential option for single men. Once home to members of Detroit Tigers baseball, and Lions football professional sports teams (even beat poet Jack Kerouac haunted its corridors for a few months), the hotel ruins endure on East Jefferson at Lenox as a lasting, enigmatic relic — not unlike old, scratched up Mellow 78s — of 20th century Detroit.

THE END

---

7. Other "Universal" recording companies had no affiliation with Shoun's Detroit studio. In his obituaries, Shoun's name appeared incorrectly, with an "L" initial for his middle name — an honest mistake, considering his widow headed a memorial card provided to visitors at his funeral with "Umbra (Louie) Shoun." "Detroit-Area Obituaries," *Detroit Free Press* (January 11, 1955. Vol. 124, No. 251), 11. "Obituaries," *Detroit News* (January 10, 1955), 19. "Deaths," *Detroit Times* (January 10, 1955), 9.

post script

On July 26, 1938, after seventeen years living in America, tamburitza musician John Dobranich celebrated a new beginning as a proud citizen of the United States with a performance in Detroit of Croatian and Serbian music. Born in 1901 in Svarca, south of Karlovac in the Austro-Hungarian Empire (modern day Croatia), Dobranich joined his father in Saint Louis, Missouri, in 1921, after the Kingdom of Serbs, Croats and Slovenes was established in the aftermath of World War I.

Dobranich labored in construction during the day, and played traditional tamburitza music in the evenings with others from his birth country, eventually joining a tamburitza choir (musicians who played insruments and sang as a group) in East Saint Louis, Illinois. In 1926 he moved to Chicago, and established the Zora (meaning "sunrise," or "the dawning") Tamburitza Choir with four others. They recorded five numbers for Victor Records' ethnic music series in 1929, the year Dobranich's homeland adopted the name Yugoslavia.[1]

Zora Tamburitza Choir traveled America's back roads to perform for Slavic people working in mining and logging communities across Colorado, Wyoming, Montana, Minnesota, and Wisconsin. Dobranich married, and from Chicago he moved to Superior, Wisconsin, where the Zora choir performed its passionate harmonies for four years.

---

1. Biographical information from anonymous liner notes printed on the record album sleeve for "To Remember Zora," Zora Record Company, Z-101 (date unknown).

In 1934, Dobranich and his wife settled in a house on Detroit's east side. He worked at Budd Wheel Company on Charlevoix Street, north of the Chrysler plant, earned his citizenship, and promoted Croation and Serbian music. In 1940, Dobranich received copyrights for a new record company called Zora.[2] Although precise dates of about twenty 78s and one long-play album are unknown, Dobranich's enterprise coincided with that of Louie Shoun, Harry Graham, and Ed Kiely.[3]

Besides his tamburitza choir, Dobranich recorded other Croatian, and Serbian acts based in the Midwest. In March 1941, *Billboard* announced Dobranich was in business to sell records to juke box operators.[4]

The war interrupted Zora productions, but in July 1949, *Billboard* reported Dobranich was preparing to get his music "back on the market after a long absence."[5] And then, nothing.

Dobranich may have drawn a curtain over his ambitions, after his name appeared in a 1949 investigation by the Un-American Activities Commission in Washington, D.C. During those years of anti-communist agitation, the commission examined the American

---

2. Dobranich's business was referred to as Zora Recording Studios, as well as the Zora Record Company.
3. The Zora record label design included similarities to Universal, Hot Wax, and Mellow labels, with hand-drawn illustrations, and hand-scribed information.
4. "Amusement Machines," *Billboard* (March 15, 1941. Vol. 53, No. 11), 75.
5. "Talent and Tunes on Music Machines," *Billboard* (July 2, 1949. Vol. 61, No. 27), 117.

Slav Congress, and associated organizations. The 1950 publication of the commission's findings included a comprehensive state-by-state list of chapters, including the names of Detroit members.[6]

After World War II ended, Yugoslavia was absorbed into the bloc of East European countries under the influence of the Soviet Union and its political system. The Un-American Activities Commission reported finding evidence of pro-communist messages sent from Yugoslavia, and Russia, to the leaders of the American Slav Congress. At the time, what other kinds of messages would Soviet authorities allow to leave those places?

Other than a commemorative twelve-inch record album of twelve Zora recordings, probably assembled during the 1960s, with liners written in Croat, and produced without contact information, Dobranich seemingly dropped off the face of the Earth.[7]

In reality, he and his wife moved to peaceful Newaygo Michigan, a village on the Muskegon River where, under the canopy of the Huron-Manistee National Forests, he could wander the woods, listening to the music in his heart each morning, as the sun shown over the water.

---

6. Un-American Activities Commission, *Report on the American Slav Congress and Associated Organizations*, June 26, 1949. United States: U.S. Government Printing Office, 1950.

7. Another tamburitza choir called "Zora," based in Gary, Indiana, was active from the 1950s through the late 20th century. Southeast Michigan is home to the Detroit Tamburitza Orchestra, first organized in 1957, and still active today.

POST SCRIPT

discographies

Master numbers presented at left. Missing numbers unknown at time of publication.

Important street addresses
12942 East Jefferson Avenue — *Universal Recording Studios; Universal Record Company*
965 Dickerson Avenue — *Universal, Hot Wax, and Mellow record companies; Mellow Music Shop (No. 2); Shoun Radio and TV Service; Globe Music Company*
519 Lenox Avenue — *Kiely's home address, used for Universal Record Company (after 12942 E. Jefferson, and before 965 Dickerson)*
13217 East Jefferson Avenue — *Mellow Music Shop (No. 1)*

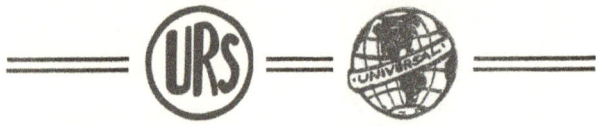

Section I: Universal Recording Studios

12942 East Jefferson Avenue
Detroit, Michigan

101......... "Toward The Stream" — Heidelberg Eight — Polka — Michael Pesamoska: Clarinet lead; Robert Howell: Cornet; Reginald Jones: Cornet; Frank F. Odziana: Clarinet; Andy Bagozzi: Trombone; Benny Netzloff: Baritone; Jos. Gazarek: Horn; Andy Schemmel: Bass; Jack Ladzinski: Drums [1939; Issued with 102]

102......... "The Leader" — Heidelberg Eight — Waltz [1939; Issued with 101; For personnel, see 101]

105......... "Hamtramck Mama" — Words and Lyrics by York Bros. — Hillbilly - Novelty; Distributed by Marquette Music

Co., Detroit [1939; George and Leslie York; three varieties of labels: Marquette Music Company=blue, red; Universal Record Co.=red; Issued with 106; also with 405 on Hot Wax, and Mellow]

106......... "Going Home" — By York Bros. — Hillbilly - Novelty [1939; George and Leslie York; Issued with 105]

107......... "Highland Park Girl" — Words and Lyrics by York Bros. — Hillbilly - Novelty — Manufactured by Universal Record Co. 12942 E. Jefferson Ave - Detroit [circa 1940; George and Leslie York — includes steel guitar; Issued with 108]

108......... "Detroit Hulu Girl" — Words and Lyrics by York Bros. — Hillbilly - Novelty — Manufactured by Universal Record Co. 12942 E. Jefferson Ave - Detroit [ca. 1940; George and Leslie York — includes steel guitar; Issued with 107]

111......... "Please, Mr. President!" — Vocal: Earl Gilson — Words and Lyrics by E. Kiely and Bernie Rose; Patriotic - Dance March; Manufactured by Universal Record Co. 519 Lenox Ave. - Detroit [ca. 1940; Issued with 112]

112......... "You'll Never Be Forgotten" — Vocal: Jack Campbell — Words and Lyrics by Bernie Rose; Vocal - Ballad; Manufactured by Universal Record Co. 519 Lenox Ave. - Detroit [ca. 1940; Issued with 111]

114......... "She Won't Turn Over For Me" — Chick Fowler's Band, Vocal: Chick Fowler — Vocal - Novelty; Manufactured by Universal Record Co. 519 Lenox Ave. - Detroit [ca. 1940; Issued with 115]

115......... "My Dream" — Chick Fowler's Band, Vocal: Earl Gilson — Fox-Trot, Vocal Chorus; Manufactured by Universal Record Co. 519 Lenox Ave. - Detroit [ca. 1940; Issued with 114]

Records with second Universal label design (red paper, gold ink, except 1002 printed with silver ink):

116......... "Just A Closer Walk With Thee" — Bethany "Cho" Ebenezer Church Directed By Elizabeth Gary; Featuring Mildred Wallace [ca. 1940; Issued with 117]

117......... "Until I Found The Lord" — Bethany "Cho" Ebenezer Church Directed By Elizabeth Gary; Featuring Odella Robinson / Mina Madkins [ca. 1940; Issued with 116]

118......... "He's My Rock My Shield" — Bethany "Cho" Ebenezer Church Directed By Elizabeth Gary; Featuring Odella Robinson [ca. 1940; Issued with 119]

119......... "Have A Little Talk With Jesus" — Bethany "Cho" Ebenezer Church Directed By Elizabeth Gary; Dedicated To The Rev. Baber [ca. 1940; Issued with 118]

126......... "Conscription Blues" — York Bros. — Hillbilly - Novelty [ca. 1940; George and Leslie York; Issued with 402 (Universal), also on Rialto (*see Section VI*)]

127......... "That Nagging Young Husey" [sp.] — York Bros. — Hillbilly - Novelty [ca. 1940; George and Leslie York; Issued with 105 on Hot Wax (*see below*)]

128......... "Victory March – U. of D. Anthem" — Tower-St. Francis Glee Club — University of Detroit [ca. 1940]

129......... "Dear Old U. of D.   U. of D. Stein Song" — Tower-St. Francis Glee Club — University of Detroit [ca. 1940]

402......... "Gamblers Blues" — York Bros. — Hillbilly - Novelty — Manufactured by Universal Record Co., 965 Dickerson Ave. Detroit [ca. 1940; George and Leslie York — includes steel guitar; Issued with 126 (Universal)]

404......... "Sweetheart Darling" [Copyright 1943 by Dixie Publishing Co. as "Speak To Me Little Darling," as recorded for Decca 5933] — York Bros. [ca. 1940; George and Leslie York — includes steel guitar; Issued with 405 (Universal)]

405......... "It Tain't No Good" — York Bros. — Hillbilly - Novelty — [ca. 1940; George and Leslie York — includes steel guitar; Issued with 404 (Universal), 105 (Hot Wax, Mellow) and 1105 (Mellow)]

1002-A .. "Snake Bite Blues" — Rye's Red River Blue Yodlers; Vocal: Conrad Brooks [Forest Rye] — Hillbilly - Novelty — Universal Record Co. 965 Dickerson Ave., Detroit [ca. 1941]

1002-B ... "Don't Come Crying Around Me Mama" — Rye's Red River Blue Yodlers; Vocal: Conrad Brooks [Forest Rye] — Hillbilly - Novelty — Universal Record Co. 965 Dickerson Ave., Detroit [ca. 1941]

Section II: Hot Wax

965 Dickerson Avenue
Detroit, Michigan

Paired entries represent one commercial disc.

Red label with gold ink:

105......... "Hamtramck Mama" — By York Bros. — Hillbilly - Novelty — Manufactured by Mellow Record Shop, 965 Dickerson, Detroit [1939; Universal master]

127......... "That Nagging Young Husey" [sp.] — By York Bros. — Hillbilly - Novelty — Manufactured by Mellow Record Shop, 965 Dickerson, Detroit [ca. 1940; Universal master]

1615-A .. "Trifling On Me" — Billy Casteel with Silver Sage Buckaroo's [sp.] — Hillbilly - Novelty — Manufactured by Mellow Record Co., 965 Dickerson Ave., Detroit, Michigan [1942; Issued with 1615-B]

1615-B .. "I Wish I Had Never Met You" — Billy Casteel with Silver Sage Buckaroo's — Hillbilly - Novelty — Manufactured by Mellow Record Co., 965 Dickerson Ave., Detroit, Michigan [1942; Issued with 1615-A]

1616-A .. "You Had Time To Think It Over" — Rye's Red River Blue Yodlers; Vocal: Conrad Brooks [Forest Rye] — Hillbilly - Blues — Manufactured by Mellow Record Co., 965 Dickerson Ave., Detroit, Michigan [1942; Issued with 1616-B]

1616-B .. "On Down The Line" — Rye's Red River Blue Yodlers; Vocal: Conrad Brooks [Forest Rye] — Hillbilly - Blues — Manufactured by Mellow Record Co., 965 Dickerson Ave., Detroit, Michigan [1942; Issued with 1616-A]

Black label with silver ink:

105......... "Hamtramck Mama" — By York Bros. — Hillbilly - Novelty — Manufactured by Mellow Record Co., 965 Dickerson Ave., Detroit, Michigan [1939; Universal master; also pressed without Mellow address, but with: Distributed by Buhl Sons Co.]

405......... "It Tain't No Good" — By York Bros. — Hillbilly - Novelty — Manufactured by Mellow Record Co., 965 Dickerson Ave., Detroit, Michigan [ca. 1940; Universal master; also pressed without Mellow address, but with: Distributed by Buhl Sons Co.]

1614-A .. "Hollywood Mama" — Billy Casteel with Silver Sage Buckaroo's — Hillbilly - Novelty — Manufactured by Mellow Record Co., 965 Dickerson Ave., Detroit, Michigan [ca. 1941-42; Issued with 1614-B]

1614-B .. "Wayne County Blues" — Billy Casteel with Silver Sage Buckaroo's — Hillbilly - Novelty; Manufactured by Mellow Record Co., 965 Dickerson Ave., Detroit, Michigan [ca. 1941-42; Issued with 1614-A; Mentioned in *Billboard* magazine July 1941]

1616-A .. "You Had Time To Think It Over" — Rye's Blue Yodelers — Hillbilly - Novelty — Manufactured by Mellow Record Co., 965 Dickerson Ave., Detroit, Michigan [May 18, 1942; Issued with 1616-B]

1616-B .. "On Down The Line" — Rye's Blue Yodelers — Hillbilly - Novelty — Manufactured by Mellow Record Co., 965 Dickerson Ave., Detroit, Michigan [May 18, 1942; Issued with 1616-A]

1617-A .. "Prairie Sweetheart" — Evelyn Haire and Her Swingtime Cowgirls — Hillbilly - Novelty — Distributed by Buhl Sons Co. [1942; Issued with 1617-B]

1617-B .. "I Have Done You Wrong" — Evelyn Haire and Her Swingtime Cowgirls — Hillbilly - Novelty — Distributed by Buhl Sons Co. [1942; Issued with 1617-A]

1618-A .. "Triflin' Woman" — Evelyn Haire and Her Swingtime Cowgirls — Hillbilly - Novelty — Distributed by Buhl Sons Co. [1942; Issued with 1618-B]

1618-B .. "My Pals, My Pinto And I" — Evelyn Haire and Her Swingtime Cowgirls — Hillbilly - Novelty — Distributed by Buhl Sons Co. [1942; Issued with 1618-A]

Section III: Mellow Record Company

965 Dickerson Avenue[1]
Detroit, Michigan

Except for 1638-A/B, labels were made with silver ink on black paper; most included: "Manufactured by the Mellow Record Co. 965 Dickerson Ave. Detroit, Mich. / Distributed by Buhl Sons Co. / Detroit, Grand Rapids, Toledo"

Paired entries represent one commercial disc.

1616-A .. "You Had Time To Think It Over" — Rye's Blue Yodelers — Hillbilly - Novelty [May 18, 1942; Issued with 1616-B]

1616-B .. "On Down The Line" — Rye's Blue Yodelers — Hillbilly - Blues [May 18, 1942; Issued with 1616-A]

1617-A .. "My Prairie Sweetheart" — Eveline[sp.] Haire and Her Swingtime Cowgirls — Western Blues [1942; Issued with 1617-B]

1617-B .. "I Have Done You Wrong" — Eveline Haire and Her Swingtime Cowgirls — Hillbilly Blues [1942; Issued with 1617-A]

---

1. Evidence suggests Edward Kiely operated the Mellow Music Shop at 965 Dickerson Avenue before he opened another store at 13217 East Jefferson Avenue around 1943-44. For a few years during the mid-1940s, he promoted two shops. In 1947, Globe Music replaced Mellow at 965 Dickerson.

1618-A .. "Triflin' Woman" — Eveline Haire and Her Swingtime Cowgirls — Hillbilly Novelty — Distributed by Buhl Sons Co. [1942; Issued with 1618-B]

1618-B .. "My Pal, My Pinto And I" — Eveline Haire and Her Swingtime Cowgirls — Hillbilly Novelty — Distributed by Buhl Sons Co. [1942; Issued with 1618-A]

York Brothers records on Mellow [2]

Codes for deciphering York Brothers recordings

[*] George York: vocal, acoustic guitar; Leslie York: vocal, electrically amplified standard guitar

[•] George York: vocal, acoustic guitar; Leslie York: vocal, electrically amplified standard guitar; unknown, bass (probably Johnnie Lavender)

[#] George York: vocal, acoustic guitar; Leslie York: vocal, electrically amplified standard guitar; Johnnie Lavender: bass

(43) Copyright 1943 Dixie Music Publishing Co., 1674 Broadway, New York, NY / BMI

(44) Copyright 1944 Dixie Music Publishing Co., 1674 Broadway, New York, NY / BMI

(45) Copyright 1945 Dixie Music Publishing Co., 1674 Broadway, New York, NY / BMI

Note: When different from title on record labels, the song publisher's title as printed in commercial folios follows "Dixie Pub:" inside box brackets.

---

2. This book accounts for forty-five York Brothers recordings (including seven not pressed on two-sided commercial disks), and twenty-five two-sided commercial discs issued with Universal, Hot Wax, Mellow, Rialto, and Fortune labels (not including second or third pressings of some). Thanks to Hillbilly Researchers Dave Sax, Phil Tricker, and Al Turner for publishing a York Brothers discography some years ago, which served as an inspiration for this.

DISCOGRAPHIES 117

105......... "Hamtramck Mama" — By York Bros. [1939; Universal master]

405......... "It Taint[sp.] No Good" — By York Bros. [ca. 1940; Universal master]

1619-A .. "Blue Skies Turned To Gray" (Leslie York) — York Bros.* [1942]

1619-B .. "I Don't Want No Part Of You" (Leslie York) — York Bros.* [1942 (43)]

1620-A .. "I'll Be Happy Again" (Leslie York) — York Bros.* [1942 (43)]

1620-B .. "Goodbye And Luck To You" (Leslie York) — York Bros.* [1942 (43)]

1621-A .. "Long Gone" (Leslie York) — York Bros.* [1942 (43)]

1621-B .. "Just Wanting You" (Leslie York) — York Bros.* [1942 (43)]

1622-A .. "Hail, Hail Ol' Glory!" (Leslie York) — York Bros.* [1942 (43)]

1622-B .. "Riding And Singing My Song" (Leslie York) — York Bros.* [1942 (43)]

1623-A .. "Hillbilly Rose" (Leslie York) — York Bros.* [1942 (43)]

1623-B .. "If I Would Never Lose You" [Dixie Pub: "If I Knew I Would Never Lose You"] (Leslie York) — York Bros.* [1942 (43)]

1624-A .. "Going Back To The Sunny South" [Dixie Pub: "Going Back To The Sunny West"] (Leslie York) — York Bros.* [1942 (45)]

1624-B .. "Life Can Never Be The Same" (Leslie York) — York Bros.* [1942 (43)]

1625-A .. "We're Gonna Catch That Train" [Dixie Pub: "Gonna Catch That Train"] (Leslie York) — York Bros.* [1942 (43)]

1625-B .. "It Makes Me Jealous Hearted" [Dixie Pub: "Jealous Hearted Blues"] (George York) — York Bros.* [1942 (43)]

1629 .... "Home In Old Tennessee" [Dixie Pub: "In Old Tennessee"] — York Bros.• [1942 (43); Source possibly a one-sided disc]

1105 .... "Hamtramck Mama" — York Bros.• [1942]

405 .... "It Taint[sp.] No Good" — By York Bros. [ca. 1940; Universal master]

1633-A .. "Memories Of You" (Leslie York) — York Bros.• [1942 (44)]

1633-B .. "New Trail To Mexico" (Leslie York) — York Bros.• [1942 (43)]

1634-A .. "Rose Of The Rio Grande" (Leslie York) — York Bros.• [1942 (43)]

1634-B .. "York Brothers Blues" (George York) — York Bros.• [1942]

1635-A .. "Kentucky's Calling Me" (Leslie York) — York Bros.• [1942 (45)]

1635-B .. "Got To Get Rid Of My Worried Mind" [Dixie Pub: "Gotta Get Rid Of My Worried Mind Somehow"] (Leslie York) — York Bros.• [1942 (44)]

1636....... "I Told The Moon About You" (Leslie York) — York Bros. [1942; Source possibly a one-sided disc]

1637-A .. "Maybe Then You'll Care" [Dixie Pub: "Maybe Then You Will Care"] — York Bros.• [1942 (44)]

1637-B .. "You Stayed Away Too Long" — York Bros.• [1942 (43)]

1638-A .. "Going To The Shindig" — York Brothers# — 13217 East Jefferson Avenue, Detroit, Mich. [1942; Red paper and gold ink; No reference to Buhl Sons Co.]

1638-B .. "Mother's Sunny Smile" — York Brothers# — 13217 East Jefferson Avenue, Detroit, Mich. [1942 (45); Red paper and gold ink; No reference to Buhl Sons Co.]

1640-A .. "A Merry Christmas To The Boys Over There" (Leslie York) — By York Bros. and Jonnie[sp.] Lavender# [1942; Issued with Mellow 1641-B]

1641-B .. "Not Over Thirty-Five" (Leslie York) — By York Bros. and Jonnie Lavender# [1942; Issued with Mellow 1640-A; Mentioned in *Billboard* magazine December 1942]

1642-A .. "I Got My Eyes On You" (George York) — By York Bros. and Jonnie Lavender# [1942]

1642-B .. "You'll Pay For It All" (Leslie York) — York Bros. and Jonnie Lavender# [1942 (44)]

Section IV: "Property of Mellow Record Co."

One-sided vinyl discs — possibly test/reference pressings or juke box promotional records

The following records represent one-sided 78 rpm discs with white paper labels and hand-written information (master numbers were also etched into deadwax areas). Text on white paper labels typically included "Property of Mellow Record Co.", along with song title, artist and master number. Reverse of one disc was stamped, "Mellow Record Co. / 965 Dickerson Ave., / Phone Murray 747 / Detroit, Mich." Commercial pressings of the 1660 series, and 2001-A do not exist.

1616-A .. "You Had Time To Think It All Over" [released as "You Had Time To Think It Over"] — Rye's Red River Blue Yodlers —Dated "May 18, 42'" [Same take issued on disc paired with 1616-B.]

1616-B .. "On Down The Line" — Rye's Red River Blue Yodlers — Dated "May 18, 42'" [Same take issued on disc paired with 1616-A.]

1617-A .. "Prairie Sweetheart" — Evelyn Haire and Her Swingtime Cowgirls [1942; Same take issued on disc paired with 1617-B.]

Symbol glossary for York Brothers recordings
[#] George York: vocal, acoustic guitar; Leslie York: vocal, electrically amplified standard guitar; Johnnie Lavender, bass

[•] George York: vocal, acoustic guitar; Leslie York: vocal, electrically amplified standard guitar; unknown: bass (probably Johnnie Lavender)

(44) Copyright 1944 Dixie Music Publishing Co., 1674 Broadway, New York, NY / BMI

Note: When different from title on record labels, the song publisher's title as printed in commercial folios follows "Dixie Pub:" inside box brackets.

1642-A .. "I Got My Eyes On You" — York Bros.# [1942; Same take issued on disc paired with 1642-B.]

1662-A .. "The Stars In Heaven" (Leslie York) — York Bros.• [ca. 1943 (44)]

1662-B .. "The Execution" — York Bros.• [ca. 1943]

1664-A .. "There's No Stars In Heaven" [Dixie Pub: "Tomorrow Brings Memories"] — York Bros.• [ca. 1943 (44)]

1665-B ... "Hula Girl Wobble" — York Bros.• [Instrumental; ca. 1943; Performance led by steel guitar, possibly played by Leslie York]

1666-A .. "You Lied To Me" [Dixie Pub: "You're Going Away"] — York Bros.• [Vocal: George York; ca. 1943 (44)]

2001-A .. "High And Dry" — Mary Cuttler[sp?] [ca. 1942-44; Novelty song with vocal, fiddle, rhythm guitar, and string bass]

Section V: Other York Brothers songs printed in books by Dixie Music Publishing

"I'll Always Care For You" (Leslie York) 1945 [*Songs of the Mountains and Prairies — Book 4*; No recording known to exist]

"I'll Love You Always" (Leslie York) 1944 [*Songs of the Mountains and Prairies — Book 1*; No recording known to exist]

"My Little Honeysuckle Rose" (Leslie York) 1944 [*Songs of the Mountains and Prairies — Book 6*; Decca 6018 (1942)]

"My Love For You Will Never Die" (Leslie York) 1944 [*Songs of the Mountains and Prairies — Book 1*; No recording known to exist]

"New Mississippi River Blues" (Leslie York) 1944 [*Songs of the Mountains and Prairies — Book 6*; King 766 (1949)]

"Nobody But Me" (George York) 1944 [*Songs of the Mountains and Prairies — Book 1*; No recording known to exist]

"Roundup Way Out Yonder" (Leslie York) 1944 [*Songs of the Mountains and Prairies — Book 1*; No recording known to exist]

Section VI: Universal masters reissued by Fortune Records

11629 Linwood Street
Detroit, Michigan

1949

Rialto R-118 A .. "You Are My Sunshine" — Cliff and His Cowboys [Hillbilly] (*see chapter 16*)

Rialto R-118 B .. "Calling Me" [Reissue of "Conscription Blues" Universal 126] — York Bros. [Hillbilly Novelty]

Fortune 120 ..... "Hamtramck Mama" — York Bros. [Universal 105; another Fortune pressing misspelled title as "Hamtramack Mama"]

Fortune 120 ..... "Highland Park Girl" — York Bros. [Universal 107]

1954

Fortune 180 ..... "Detroit Hula Girl" — York Bros. [Universal 108]

Fortune 180 ..... "Going Home" — York Bros. [Universal 106]

Section VII: Possible Universal Recording Studios productions

Paired entries represent one commercial disc.

The Four Dukes — Distributed by Buhl Sons Company / Detroit - Toledo / Grand Rapids; Labels made of silver ink on black paper; Label designed in hand-drawn style similar to Universal/Hot Wax/Mellow labels; Four-digit master numbers in end wax similar to those stamped in Universal records.

6500....... "Mammy's Little Blackout Baby" (G. Moriarty - M. Moriarty) — The Four Dukes - Vocal Quartette — Peaka Record Co. Detroit, Mich. — Distributed by Buhl Sons Company / Detroit - Toledo - Grand Rapids [1942; Issued with 6501]

6501....... "You're Gonna Win That Ball Game Uncle Sam" (G. Moriarty - C. Bonner) — The Four Dukes - Vocal Quartette — Words by George Moriarty and music by Carl Bonner — Distributed by Buhl Sons Company / Detroit - Toledo - Grand Rapids [1942; Issued with 6500]

Charlie Jones and his Kentucky Corn Crackers — Note use of four-digit master numbers, similar to Mellow's 1600 series.

1782-A .. "Honey, You Can't Fool Me Anymore" (Bill Hicks) Vocal: Bill Hicks — Kentucky Corn Crackers [ca. 1947; Issued on Arcadia 1782A; Vargo 29029]

1782-B .. "Dodge Street Waltz" (Charlie Jones) — Kentucky Corn Crackers [Instrumental; ca. 1947; Issued on Arcadia 1782B; Vargo 29029]

1783-A .. "My Dreams Of You Cannot Come True" (Bill Hicks) Vocal: Bill Hicks — Kentucky Corn Crackers [ca. 1947; Issued on Arcadia 1783A; Vargo 29028]

1783-B .. "Kentucky Rag" (Charlie Jones) — Kentucky Corn Crackers [Instrumental; ca. 1947; Issued on Arcadia 1783B; Vargo 29028]

1784-A .. "Stony Point" — Charlie Jones and his Kentucky Corn Crackers [Instrumental; ca. 1947; Issued on Vargo 29032A, Rondo R-170-A]

1784-B .. "Ida Red" — Charlie Jones and his Kentucky Corn Crackers [Instrumental; ca. 1947; Issued on Vargo 29032B, Rondo R-170-B]

1785-A .. "Gray Eagle" — Charlie Jones and his Kentucky Corn Crackers [Instrumental; ca. 1948; Issued on Vargo 29033A, Rondo R-169-A]

1785-B .. "Pulling The Bow" — Charlie Jones and his Kentucky Corn Crackers [Instrumental; ca. 1948; Issued on Vargo 29033B, Rondo R-169-B]

1786-A .. "New San Antonio Rose" (Bob Wills) Vocal: Geo. Sikes Trio — Charlie Jones and his Kentucky Corn Crackers [ca. 1948; Issued on Vargo 29048A]

1786-B .. "Barbara Polka" Accordion: Micky Wionesk — Charlie Jones and his Kentucky Corn Crackers [Instrumental; ca. 1948; Issued on Vargo 29048B, Rondo R-165-B]

1787-A .. "Snow Deer" — Charlie Jones and his Kentucky Corn Crackers [Instrumental; ca. 1948; Issued on Vargo 29049A, Rondo R-168-B]

1787-B .. "Old Dan Tucker" — Charlie Jones and his Kentucky Corn Crackers [Instrumental; ca. 1948; Issued on Vargo 29049B, Rondo R-168-A]

1788-A .. "Cool Water" (Bob Nolan) Vocal: Geo. Sikes Trio — Charlie Jones and his Kentucky Corn Crackers [ca. 1948; Issued on Vargo 29050B]

1788-B .. "Sweet Georgie[sp.] Brown" Electric Guitar: Bob Turner — Charlie Jones and his Kentucky Corn Crackers [Instrumental; ca. 1948; Issued on Vargo 29050A, Rondo R-152-B]

1789-A .. "I Want A Girl" Vocal: Geo Sikes Trio — Charlie Jones and his Kentucky Corn Crackers [ca. 1948; Issued on Vargo 29051, Rondo R-152-A]

1789-B .. "Dark Town Strutters Ball" Electric Guitar: Bob Turner — Charlie Jones and his Kentucky Corn Crackers [Instrumental; ca. 1948; Issued on Vargo 29051, Rondo R-165-A]

Elton Adams and his Blue Ridge Mountaineers — Note use of four-digit master numbers, similar to Mellow's 1600 series.

1802....... "Philipino Waltz" — Elton Adams and his Blue Ridge Mountaineers [Instrumental; ca. 1948; Issued on Vargo 29027, Rondo R-162-A]

1803....... "Silver Bells" — Elton Adams and his Blue Ridge Mountaineers [Instrumental; ca. 1948; Issued on Vargo 29027, Rondo R-162-B]

1804....... "E Blues" (Red Nix) Vocal: Red Nix — Elton Adams and his Blue Ridge Mountaineers [ca. 1948; Issued on Arcadia 184-6, Vargo 29026]

1806....... "Good Old Mountain Dew" (Horace W. Hall) Vocal: Red Nix and Elton Adams — Elton Adams and his Blue Ridge Mountaineers [ca. 1948; Issued on Arcadia 184-6, Vargo 29026]

acknowledgments

Without generous attention from the following people, this work would not exist: John Bell, Keith Cady, Loney Charles, Kevin Coffey, Kevin Fontenot, Nathan D. Gibson, Paul Gifford, Carolyn Gnagy, Lucas Hartwell, Michael Hurtt, Steven Lapinsky, Lea Ann Nall-Williams, Gary Oatsvall, Carl Pellegrino, Adam Stanfel, and George York; as well as Ed Kiely's grandnephew, and a grandson of Louie Shoun. My sincere respect to all.

My thanks to these taxpayer- and member-supported institutions: the National Archives at Kansas City, the Archives of Michigan, the Library of Michigan, the Detroit Historical Society, and the Baldwin Public Library of Birmingham, Michigan.

Finally, my love and gratitude to my wife and family.

www.ingramcontent.com/pod-product-compliance
Lightning Source LLC
Chambersburg PA
CBHW031137090426
42738CB00008B/1126